Room
for
Improvement

THE POST-COLLEGE GIRL'S
GUIDE TO ROOMMATE LIVING

Amy Zalneraitis

SIMON SPOTLIGHT ENTERTAINMENT
New York London Toronto Sydney

Acknowledgments

Many thanks to my agent, Billy Kingsland at Kuhn Projects; my editor, Emily Westlake; my "proofreader," Andy McLaughlin; my favorite neighborhood bar, Daddy O's, where I often sought refuge from roommates; my family and friends, especially all the "anonymous" friends whose stories made this book possible; the experts who provided me with invaluable advice and insight for this book, Dr. Ella Lasky, Dr. Barbara Lewis, Dr. Kevin Kulic, and Dr. Harold Pass; and every roommate I've ever had.

S|S|E

SIMON SPOTLIGHT ENTERTAINMENT
An imprint of Simon & Schuster
1230 Avenue of the Americas, New York, New York 10020
Text copyright © 2008 by Amy Zalneraitis

SIMON SPOTLIGHT ENTERTAINMENT and related logo are trademarks of
Simon & Schuster, Inc.
Designed by Gabe Levine
Manufactured in the United States of America
First Edition
2 4 6 8 10 9 7 5 3 1
Library of Congress Cataloging-in-Publication Data
Zalneraitis, Amy.
Room for improvement : the post-college girl's guide to roommate
living / by Amy Zalneraitis.—1st ed.
p. cm.
Includes bibliographical references and index.
ISBN-13: 978-1-4169-5089-9
ISBN-10: 1-4169-5089-3
1. Roommates—United States. 2. Shared housing—United States.
3. Young women—United States—Life skills guides. I. Title.
HQ975.5.Z35 2008
646.70088'363594220973—dc22
2007025608

Table of Contents

Introduction

Since moving to New York City more than seven years ago, I have spent a considerable amount of time venting about living with roommates—the everyday problems, the precarious circumstances, and the seemingly endless crazy behavior. I found that my girlfriends and I could sit around for hours talking about our living situations, mainly because these conversations were cathartic for us—spontaneous therapy sessions that taught us we weren't the only ones dealing with a roommate who shamelessly stole our socks on a weekly basis or flirted *just a little too much* with our boyfriends. What we didn't talk about as we swapped stories of horrific roommate behavior is the fact that in almost every sense of the word, we felt like adults—we had "real" jobs, we were more attached to our political beliefs and moral views than we'd ever been, and we were more selective about the people we chose to hang out with—but something was keeping us from fully feeling like we had reached adulthood, and that was our living situations.

If we didn't happen to live in major cosmopolitan (that is, too-expensive-to-afford-to-rent-our-own-one-bedroom-apartments) cities, we probably wouldn't have been living with one or more other people. But living solo was and continues to be an unrealistic expectation for most twentysomethings who reside in cities such as New York. In fact, Manhattan rental properties are more than 99 percent occupied, according to the *New York Post*, meaning that the competition is fierce and the desperation very real for those looking for a good roommate in a good apartment. According to a CNNMoney.com article, the three priciest rental markets are New York City (with an average rent of $2,553), San Francisco ($1,685), and Boston ($1,632), which are—not coincidentally—among the most alluring cities for young, ambitious people. Other cities or regions in the top ten include New Haven, Connecticut ($1,485); Orange County, California ($1,458); San Jose, California ($1,445); Northern New Jersey ($1,404); Los Angeles, California ($1,360); Oakland, California ($1,262); and San Diego, California ($1,250).

Plain and simple, in order to afford living in some of the most desirable cities, most of us have to resign ourselves to living with roommates. Though often necessary, living with roommates after a certain age can feel unnatural. As we continue to grow as individuals (move up in our careers, develop more stable relationships, both platonic and romantic, and graduate from keg parties to cocktail parties), we are still stuck living as if we were in college housing, agonizing over things like why one roommate always has to bring the party home or why another seems to monopolize the bathroom only on mornings when you're in a mad rush. I know from my own experience that the majority of people in their twenties and thirties who have roommates aren't thrilled with the idea. We thought that by this age, we'd be living alone or with a romantic partner (who, of course, can present some of the same "living together" problems, but somehow their offenses are more forgivable), or maybe we'd even own something. But management company Citi Habitats's latest Black and White Report revealed that the average renter in New York is thirty years old—not surprising considering the average price of a co-op is $1.109 million. What twentysomething, save one with an enormous trust fund, can afford to buy in a market like this?

The stories my girlfriends and I would constantly share, compounded by the rental climate, made me realize that we'd hit a cultural nerve, and it got me thinking: If books have been written on how to live comfortably with roommates in college, why are there no comprehensive guides out there on how to live with roommates *after* college, sometimes even *way after* college?

I've lived with roommates almost all my adult life, until recently, which means that by age thirty I'd had roommates— a dizzying number of them—for more than a decade. These roommates ranged from complete strangers to close friends, and they all provided material for this book. Even *my* behavior as a roommate provided fodder for this book (see Chapter One: Nobody's Perfect, Including You). Then, of course, there are the stories I've compiled from my girlfriends and their friends, coworkers, acquaintances, relatives, and girls who simply heard about the book and were dying to contribute their own experiences.

In *Room for Improvement*, I have provided you with what I hope will be useful information and roommate stories that will help you develop a more sophisticated ability to recognize when things are turning bad with your own roommate or room-mates and teach you how to take control before things turn unbearable. But remember, while advice, rules, and expert commentary are important, they're somewhat malleable. View them more as guidelines that can help you create a harmoni-ous living situation rather than as set-in-stone tenets. After all, equally crucial as preventing and rectifying apartment prob-lems is having fun and being happy while living with room-mates. Mistakes happen. We do stupid things. We get drunk and act like jerks. We get hungry late at night and eat others' food. We covet a shirt so badly that we borrow it without ask-ing. Roommates should be forgiving . . . to an extent.

I wrote this book because I've learned from my experi-ences, which in no way means that if I still lived with other girls I'd be the perfect roommate today. What it means is that had I known the things I know now, I would've made a lot of different decisions. I would've handled conflict in a more pro-ductive way and been more selective about whom I chose to live with. Some people will pick up this book because they are suffering or have suffered through bad roommate situations, others will read it to be entertained, and most will read it for a combination of the two. In some of the stories and the rules you may recognize your own bad behavior, and perhaps do something to mend your ways.

Please bear in mind as you read this that some identifying details and all names of people (and pets) in the roommate stories (except for mine and my sister's) have been changed and that some people have been split into more than one character, but all of the events and situations described— every single crazy one of them—actually occurred.

Chapter One
Nobody's Perfect, Including You

DO remember that every human being has the
capacity (and occasionally the right) to be annoying.
DON'T forget that this applies to you, too.

It's only fair that I start off with the roommate don'ts I myself
have committed over the years. Most of them consist of the
usual crimes, like helping myself to food that wasn't mine, wearing my roommates' clothes without asking, stealing quarters for
laundry (which are like gold nuggets in cities like New York,
where personal washers and dryers are virtually nonexistent),
and giving undeserved attitude to roommates simply because I
happened to be in a bad mood. Others were more serious and,
looking back, make me cringe with embarrassment. The thing
is, no matter how major or venial my sins, I usually found a way
to justify or rationalize them.

One of the worst crimes I committed was against a friend I
lived with in a tiny, dark apartment on New York City's Upper

West Side. We moved in together after a long and tumultuous relationship I was in had ended. To have called me oversensitive or emotional would have been a gross understatement. A simple "How are you?" induced crying fits, as did portrayals of couples, happy or otherwise, on TV. (At my lowest point, while watching some sort of tribute to the show *All in the Family,* I actually felt painfully jealous of Archie and Edith Bunker's relationship.) My life was riddled with associative memories, and seemingly ordinary things like the Sunday Styles section of the *New York Times* or a rotten banana (pathetic, but true) were reminders of the relationship I'd lost. I cried in the shower, in my food, on the phone, while getting dressed in the morning, on my roommate's shoulder, sometimes even in *her* food. Then I harassed her with questions like, "Do you think he misses me, like really, really misses me?" or "Do you think he's sleeping with someone else . . . right now, this minute?" That's not an exaggeration: I wanted her to tell me exactly what he was doing and thinking at any given point in the day. She did her best to pacify me, telling me what I wanted to hear. ("Yes, of course he misses you. No, he wouldn't dream of being with someone else yet. He's in as much pain as you.") But she eventually stopped responding when she realized I wasn't absorbing anything she said. Unfortunately, this didn't stop me from pleading for answers, so for nights on end she had to listen to my whining and sobbing. I'm sure she had problems and worries of her own, but I never knew what they were because I monopolized all the woe-is-me time. She even quit her job during my breakup hell, but I had completely forgotten about it until she didn't wake up at her normal time one morning.

"Aren't you going to be late?" I asked.

"For what?" she asked sleepily.

"For work," I snapped, annoyed that I had to put my self-pity on hold for even ten seconds to focus on someone else's life.

"I quit, Amy, remember?" she said, and then rolled over without waiting for a response.

When I told her I'd decided to start seeing a therapist, tears welled up in her eyes. Initially, I thought she was crying out of pity for me. I realized later they were tears of joy for her own impending freedom. Sadly, seeing a therapist did nothing to curb my complaining. Instead, I came home from my sessions and talked, ad nauseam, about what was discussed during them. I was the incarnation of Misery Loves Company, forcing my roommate to suffer through a breakup that wasn't even hers.

I also became a raging hypochondriac during this time, which may or may not have been a symptom of the breakup. To this day, I still suffer from a mild case of it.

"I'm almost positive I have lupus," I said gravely as I walked through our front door one day after work.

"What?!" my roommate asked.

"I just read an article on it, and I have all the symptoms. *All of them.*"

"Like what?"

"I don't want to talk about it," I said, tears streaming down my face. "I have to call my parents and tell them." In the months following, I erroneously diagnosed myself with everything from skin cancer to the beginning stages of Parkinson's disease, and my roommate was there to witness every one of my freak-outs.

When we finally moved out of our shared apartment, we didn't talk for a good three months. I felt like I had lost my therapist, my general physician, the only person who truly understood what I was going through. She felt like she'd been released from prison. Shockingly, we've remained friends, but that may have something to do with the fact that we were good friends before we moved in together. (When I was acting completely neurotic, she could find some solace in the memory of the person I had been prebreakup. "I always held out hope that that person would come back," she eventually told me.) But it probably has more to do with how profusely I apologized after our three-month break from each other. She also found comfort in the knowledge that the chances of us ever living together again were nil. After what I put her through, though, she had every right to cut me out of her life.

I realize now that I forced us both into roles that prevented us from having a normal relationship, as friends and roommates. I was the inconsolable whiner, and she the reluctant therapist. Psychology teaches us that we'll often try to recreate familial-type relationships in our adult lives, and roommate situations can be particularly conducive to this. It's common

for one girl to take on (or be forced into) the all-knowing/
advice-giving role while the other adapts to the naïve/needy
position, as happened in my
case. Fundamentally, neither
roommate may be as needy or all
knowing as she eventually acts,
but if roommates aren't aware
of this natural tendency to take
on these roles, they can end up
in a frustrating and unhealthy
mother-daughter-type situation.
"If you find yourself acting in a
way that's not normal for you, sit

> **Myth:** Like MTV's *The Real
> World*, roommates should be
> instantly and totally involved
> in each other's lives.
> **Fact:** People like to choose
> just how close they get to
> someone. Don't assume that
> physical closeness means
> it's okay for your problems
> to become your roommate's
> problems.

back and look at the role you're playing," says Harold Pass,
Ph.D. "And ask yourself if your roommate is eliciting this
behavior in you." In other words, if you find yourself acting
as a person you don't recognize, something is wrong with
the relationship. I was forcing my roommate into a role she
didn't want to play, a role that didn't make her happy and
that didn't represent who she truly was. It was my fault for
putting her in that position, but according to Barbara Lewis,
Ph.D., it also didn't help that she wasn't firm about creating boundaries. If you find yourself in a place similar to the
one I put my ex-roommate in, don't feel bad about saying
something to your roommate about the burden she's placing
on you. "You must establish boundaries," insists Dr. Lewis.
"It's a two-way street. You should *tell* your roommate if she's

burdening you too much, and she should *ask* you if she's burdening you too much."

Another valuable lesson I learned from my own bad roommate behavior is that you should never put your roommate in a position where she has to clean up your sticky messes, which is exceedingly easy to do when you're living under the same roof. I was the perpetrator of such a crime when I tried to get out of a romantic relationship without actually breaking up with the guy I was involved with. (To my small credit, he was impervious to all my I'm-just-not-that-into-you-anymore hints, so I knew the final breakup wasn't going to be easy.) Rather than deal with the problem head-on, I pretended it didn't exist and moved on with my love life. He, assuming we were still dating, got quite upset when I inexplicably stopped returning his calls. Being my boyfriend, he knew where I lived, so it was only a matter of time before he showed up at the apartment, demanding some sort of attention. It got particularly bad one night when, starting at 7:00 p.m., he called me seventeen times in a row, leaving ten drunken messages. Although I didn't want to face it, I knew his next step would be to show up at the apartment. I had a date that night, so rather than deal with the inevitable disaster, I spent hours picking out just the right outfit and then headed for the door.

"So . . . Chris may show up and ring the buzzer at some point tonight," I told my roommates as I checked my makeup in our hallway mirror one last time. "But just tell him I'm not here. Tell him I went to a work dinner or something." They looked at me suspiciously, but I was gone before they could ask any questions.

My date was a success, and I spent a blissful night away from home. My roommates, however, weren't so lucky.

"Chris did show up," one of my roommates told me the next morning, as she walked out of her bedroom, looking grumpy and tired. "And when we told him you weren't here, he refused to believe us and rang the buzzer for an hour straight."

"An hour *straight*," my other roommate angrily repeated. "When we finally threatened to call the police, he called us bitches and stumbled off."

My roommates were upset with me for some time after the incident. And justifiably so: They had to deal with the uncomfortable and annoying ramifications of my inability to handle things like an adult and were disgusted by my behavior. At twenty-seven years old, wasn't I mature enough to break up with someone on my own? After six months of dating, couldn't I bring myself to at least face the guy one last time to officially end things?

As annoying as I was to many of my past roommates, it didn't stop me from being disproportionately annoyed with them for smaller offenses, which is why it's important to really—I mean *really*—look at your own behavior before expressing annoyance toward your roommate. You don't like it when she uses almost the entire jar of your Whole Foods organic peanut butter? Well, ask yourself this: Have you ever finished off her carton of milk in the morning and then had the nerve to sneakily place the empty container back in the fridge? Chances are, you and your roommate are equally guilty of some less-than-stellar behavior. I've attacked a lot of roommates before taking a step back and weighing whether they really deserved it, and the results were never good. It always ended in a fight but never solved the initial problem. Try to see that even if your roommate did something to totally piss you off, it doesn't necessarily mean she is a bad person, it just means the problem needs to be addressed in an appropriate way. What's important is that both roommates have to be involved in solving it. Says Dr. Pass, "Realize that when solving problems or dealing with an issue, nobody has to be recognized as the bad guy. Try to stay positive." Sure, maybe your roommate is at fault for eating all your peanut butter. Maybe you want to call her a fat, selfish pig. But you can address the problem without vilifying her, at least to her face.

As Dr. Pass suggests, looking at your own behavior means being able to occasionally take an uncomfortable step back and view your roommate situation from as objective a place as possible. When we get used to our roles (for example, you have a serious boyfriend and your roommate is *seriously* single), it's hard to adjust to those roles suddenly changing. I resisted one such change when I was living with the two roommates who had to deal with my drunk, buzzer-ringing boyfriend. Before I unceremoniously ended things with this boyfriend, we probably used the couch and living room 90 percent more than both of my roommates, who were very single. When they were doing single-girl things, like going out for drinks after work, or hitting the gym together, or spending time in their rooms on their phones, I was on the couch with my boyfriend, watching movies, eating dinner, or, for entire lazy Sundays, reading the papers in the messiest way possible. They almost never used the TV or the couch because their lifestyles didn't offer them a lot of time to just hang out. But when one of them became serious with a guy, that changed. Now we had to compete for the living room, and this totally pissed me off. Rather than try to split the time fairly, I resisted giving up any of it. My boyfriend and I had certain TV shows we watched religiously and lists of movies we wanted to see. In fact, he'd become just as comfortable with my monopolization of the living room as I had. Without a TV or a couch, what would we do? Talk? Go for walks? Hang out in my tiny bedroom? How boring. (The anxiety that resulted from thinking about how not having complete access to a TV or couch would affect the relationship was clearly a symptom of something being, well, very wrong with the relationship, but that realization would come later.) The living room rights were so important to me that I'd run home from work just to claim my place on the couch. Once, my roommate who had the boyfriend called in sick to work, and the only thing I could think about in my cubicle all day was how she'd "won" the living room for the night because she'd gotten there first. And then I had an epiphany: I had become a total couch potato loser.

She and her boyfriend (and my single roommate, for that

matter) had just as much of a right as I did to use the living room—probably more, since I had basically cordoned it off for the past six months. I was too wrapped up in my sit-on-the-couch-every-night-because-I-have-a-boyfriend role to adjust to her lifestyle change. When I took a minute to look at how unfair and selfish I was being, I calmly stepped back from the couch. Promptly after that, I also stepped back (okay, ran away) from a romantic relationship that was way too dependent on a TV.

In all these situations, the easy route was to justify my self-ish actions, to continue doing what I was doing without thinking about how it made my roommates feel, and I took it. I made myself believe that what I was doing was right, and that what my roommates wanted was unfair to me. "Cognitive distortions are lenses we look through in order to make the world fit the way that best suits us," says Dr. Kevin Kulic. "They bend reality for us so that we see the world in a particular way. . . . At times they can be useful, but they're usually one-sided: What works to make you feel better may not work out so well for other people." I was being unfair to my roommates, and ultimately, my selfish-ness gave way to an underlying bitchiness between my room-mates and me. I could've prevented this by considering their feelings more; it would've benefited both them and me, since in the end we were all pretty miserable, no matter how hard I tried to justify my behavior.

It can be particularly difficult for girls to confront

each other about issues. We often opt instead to take the passive-aggressive route until one day our built-up resentment results in a blowup. If, instead of holding things in or drinking the rest of your roommate's milk because she ate your peanut butter, you deal with the problem appropriately and immediately, you're much more likely to have a workable relationship with your roommate in the future. Ella Lasky, Ph.D., says, "Instead of using a blaming, criticizing 'you' statement, try something like, 'I was really looking forward to having some of my peanut butter when I got home, and I was really disappointed that there was none left.'" It sounds hokey, but hokey often works.

Things to Remember

* Living together is an intimate situation, but moving in with someone doesn't mean you've been granted an instant best friend.
* If you happen to live with a close friend, don't take advantage of her friendship responsibilities. In other words, don't force her into the role of twenty-four-hour therapist.
* Be aware of the tendency to take on polarized roles that will lead to an unhealthy mother-daughter-type relationship.
* Memorize the fourth rule from the Buddha's Noble Eightfold Path: *No matter what we say, others know us*

from the way we behave. Before we criticize others, we should first see what we do ourselves. In fact, I suggest printing this rule out and hanging it conspicuously in your apartment.

Chapter Two
Three's a Crowd

DON'T opt to live with two other girls over one other girl.
If you are already in a threesome situation,
DO make decisions as a group, not as a pair.

How many roommates does it take to screw in a lightbulb? This isn't a trick question. The answer is two: one to do the screwing and one to hold the ladder. Add a third roommate to the mix and you'll have one doing the screwing and two holding the ladder—two who'll be snickering about how big your ass looks from their vantage point.

There's only one thing worse than two catty girls living together, and that's three girls living together. Triangulated roommate relationships can be downright disastrous. To start off, there's the whole "let's gang up on one roommate to create solidarity between the two of us" thing. Then there's Mother Nature's cruel joke, the one that causes all female roommates to menstruate in unison. And, finally, there's that nasty playground-worthy competition, having to do with things like guys, money, and jean sizes, that rears its head most virulently in threesome situations. And yet, even with all the bad stuff a threesome situation can yield, many girls are inexorably drawn to the size a three-roommate apartment provides, and it can seem fun to live with two other girls—as if you'll always have a buddy.

Myth: Three people can always live together amicably because, just like the characters on *Three's Company*, disparate personalities balance one another out, and usually in an amusing way.
Fact: Three people living together will almost always be more difficult than any other number of people living together because we're all prone to pairing off and leaving one person out.

I used to think the main problem with three girls living together was that it was simply too much estrogen under one roof, but it's actually not just that. It's about the two-against-one thing. Anything is better than three. Even four or five is better than three. Three just seems to beget juvenile cruelty. "Triangulation is a problem because there's always the lingering apprehension that you could be the next target," says Dr. Pass. The fear of becoming the ostracized one is strong enough to encourage roommates to keep one girl on the periphery—as the outsider, the one who's just not like "us." *Better her than me*, you think, even if it's subconsciously. Adds Dr. Kulic, "In any group social situation, people will form subgroups with those they're more comfortable with. If there is someone who stands out as different, the subgroup will then use their combined power to scapegoat and humiliate that individual. It's a way of asserting power and, unfortunately, it works."

I lived in Tribeca with two girls once who were friends and roommates with each other before I moved into the apartment. For the most part, we got along. Our different schedules didn't allow for too much interaction, but if they happened to have a qualm about the way I, say, loaded the dishwasher, or how I tied up the trash, I'd get an e-mail the next day that started off, "Maria and I have discussed this and would like for you to do [fill in the blank] differently." Their way of confronting me— with an e-mail signed by both of them rather than just one of them—made me feel as if I were getting reviewed by a board every week, and I became paranoid: Are they scrutinizing everything I do? Do they talk about how often (or infrequently) I wash my sheets? What do they say about my eating habits?

In retrospect, they probably didn't talk about me as much as I suspected, but that's exactly why a threesome living situation is inherently unhealthy. The formula is simple: Two roommates can—and generally will—build a relationship by, even slightly, ganging up on the third. The third senses this and becomes disproportionately paranoid. This phenomenon will especially affect you if you move into an apartment as the new third roommate. "It's always hard to be the new kid on the block," says Dr. Lewis. "Which is why it's important that all roommates be involved with setting the ground rules from the get-go." If two girls already live together, their rules (off-the-wall or reasonable) and etiquette (strict or nonexistent) were established long before you moved in. If you only live with one roommate, problem solving is easier: You can approach her as a person—a person who is much more likely to compromise. In a threesome apartment, where you're the third roommate, addressing a problem often feels like you're standing up to a regime. They don't need to compromise, and usually they won't. Again, as Dr. Pass says, they're inclined to keep you on the outside—the one who doesn't get *their* rules, partly because it precludes either one of them from becoming the outsider.

I was the designated outsider with the two girls who sent me the "From the Board" e-mails, and there was not a lot I could do about it, which made for some uncomfortable situations. While they were fastidious about things like keeping the apartment clean and perfectly decorated, they celebrated the end of every week like it was also the end of the world. And as I imagine is the case with most apocalyptic partying, getting completely wasted was de rigueur. Both of them were a few years older—New York City years older—than me at the time, so they had cultivated a style and level of partying I hadn't yet been exposed to. Let me give you some idea. The first Friday I moved in, I had been out with friends until about 3:00 a.m. I came home to a quiet apartment, which turned out to be quiet not because my roommates were asleep but because they hadn't yet made it home. At 4:30 a.m., I was startled out of sleep by the sound of banging at the front door. The door had no peephole, so I opened it just a crack, and standing (very unsteadily) on the other side was one of my roommates. Normally, she was a very pretty, well-put-together, impeccably dressed girl, but she now looked like a character out of a *Saturday Night Live* frat-party skit. Her mascara was smudged all over her face, and her hair looked like rats had nested in it (excuse the cliché, but after learning more about her night, there was a good chance rats *may actually have nested in it* or been in contact with it in some way), there were stains on her shirt, and she had only one arm in a fur coat that was now partially dragging on the floor behind her. Most of her words were unintelligible, but I was somehow able to gather this information from her drunken gesticulating: She'd gotten in a fight with her cab driver, then lost her keys, but "tankfahweee the fhant door wahzzzzz open." After she had gotten into the building, she had to climb five precipitous flights of stairs to our apartment. On the third floor, she stopped to rest and fell asleep. When she woke up, she had to pee so badly that she relieved herself in a random bucket in our building's hallway. With an empty bladder, the last two flights were apparently much easier to navigate because, at this point in the story, she snapped her fingers to indicate how swiftly she had climbed them. I was then forced to listen to a story about a guy she had met that night. She wanted to know if I thought he'd ever call her. "Of course," I said groggily. About fifteen minutes later my other roommate stumbled in, mumbled something about the hallway smelling like pee, drunkenly kicked off her stiletto heels (not the type of shoe that should ever be *kicked* off), shuffled into her room, and slammed the door so hard the apartment shook.

But not every Friday night in the apartment was this mellow. Typically on Friday nights, a group of people connected by their undying love for cocaine and house music descended on our apartment, and anybody in their path, including people like me who happened to live there, had three choices: join, be heckled, or leave, even if I had planned on staying in that night. The problem was, I couldn't really complain. This was their apartment before mine, and even though I was paying a portion of the rent, they had "accepted" me as their roommate, so I pretty much had to adhere to the guidelines (or lack thereof) that were in place before I came along. It sounds unfair, and it is, but it's not like there was a Human Resources department I could voice my concerns to. In fact, the one time I expressed annoyance about the thumpa-thumpa-thumping of house music blasting out of our living room at 3:00 a.m., they looked at me like I was the Reverend Shaw Moore from *Footloose*. It's not that they were mean or bitchy girls; it's just that they had already established the way fun was to be had in the apartment, and I hadn't been and would never be a part of deciding what that meant.

A threesome situation can get even screwier if you happen to get stuck living with two girls who make the Heathers[1]

---

[1] *Heathers*, the 1989 teen movie starring Christian Slater, Winona Ryder, and Shannen Doherty, is about a high school social clique (made up of Heathers I, II, and III and inductee Veronica) who terrorize the less socially fortunate around them. When Mostly (okay, maybe only Slightly) Good Veronica asks Heather III why she's such a mega brat, Heather III says, "Because I can be." Which also happens to be the mindset of most sinister roommates. Why do I steal my roommate's clothes? Because I can. Why do I hit on my roommate's boyfriend? Because I can. Why do I use my roommate's expensive shampoo and then replace it with the cheap stuff? Because I can. You get the idea.

look sweet natured. If one roommate is slightly sinister and the other one is mostly good, you're probably in okay shape. But if you're a mostly good roommate and you find yourself living with two slightly sinister ones, you're in a precarious place. There's just no way to defend oneself against evil like this. You see, a sinister roommate living with two mostly good ones won't have as much freedom to express her dark side, but put two of those fledgling demons together and they can justify just about any act. A mostly good friend of mine, Erin, learned this the hard way: She moved into a three-bedroom apartment in Brooklyn with two demon girls in their twenties. This toxic twosome pulled stuff no roommate would have the guts to pull on her own. "Money was tight for all of us," Erin said, "so borrowing each other's clothes was pretty common." Though she was poor at the time, Erin worked at a high-end clothing company, where she received an employee discount, so her closet looked more like it belonged to an Upper East Side lady who lunches rather than a girl whose bank balance regularly hit the single digits. Most weekends Erin stayed at her boyfriend's, which meant that her roommates had unrestricted access to her designer closet. "I started getting suspicious when I'd return on Sunday nights and all of a sudden they wouldn't show me any of the photos they had taken from their weekends [something they'd done when she first moved in]," Erin said. "Eventually, I stumbled on a pile of their pictures, and in every one of them they were wearing my stuff, from top to bottom! Jewelry, handbags, everything." She immediately inspected her closet.

"What I discovered was that they would remove the tags from pieces I had never even worn before and then reattach them before I came home for the weekend. There were armpit stains on my brand-new $1000 cashmere sweaters, sweaters I'd get for a discounted price or for free from work, and on sample pieces that couldn't be replaced. They were so damaged that they all had to be thrown out." Her roommates had apparently been ransacking her closet for months. Then, in what could be one of the worst sartorial crimes in history, Erin found her missing-for-weeks absolute favorite pair of jeans on the floor of one of her roommate's closets. "I was so relieved to find them, but when I put them on, they were inches too short for me. My roommate had stolen my favorite pair of jeans and gotten them tailored to fit her short, stumpy legs! She even had the nerve to get patches added to them." If Erin were a wealthy art collector, it would have been like someone had stolen one of her rare Picasso paintings, defaced it, and then thrown it in the basement. It would have been better, easier to swallow, if she had never found the jeans at all. Not only were they ruined forever, but her memory of them was ruined as well. As many girls know, a favorite pair of jeans are a one-of-a-kind, valuable piece of art. They simply can't be replaced.

If Erin had lived with just one of these girls, she probably wouldn't have lost thousands of dollars' worth of clothing. First of all, it obviously would have been harder for one girl to do the damage the two of them caused. And second, it would have been harder for someone acting alone to justify this type of behavior. In threesome situations the two slightly sinister roommates enable each other's bad behavior. The target of these bad acts is almost always the mostly good roommate. "When you're acting with someone else rather than alone," says Dr. Lewis, "it's easier to justify the bad behavior and feel better about yourself for doing it. It's like having a drinking buddy or a partner in crime: You won't feel as bad with them by your side."

My friend Simone found a partner in crime with her last roommate, Mary. When their other roommate left a disgusting mess in their communal bathroom, they got back at her in a *Heathers*-worthy way. "One night, I was chit-chatting with Mary in the bathroom while she was washing her face," Simone said. "When I glanced down at the sink, I noticed that there were black pubic hairs everywhere." Simone then screamed at Mary, who's legally blind without her glasses, to step away from the sink. "Our other roommate had apparently done some grooming *down there* and left us a present for later." Simone and Mary were grossed out and mad, and to make matters worse, when they confronted their roommate about the mess, she denied it. "She claimed she wasn't the culprit because she regularly got waxed," said Simone. So later that week, Simone and Mary did something I thought only happened in *Mean Girls*–type movies: They used her toothbrush to clean the toilet. Doing it together, they found it funny, but it's unlikely either one of them would've gone through with it without the other one by her side.

If you find yourself living with two sinister roommates, you're pretty much screwed, unless you cross over to the dark side yourself—but then you're just contributing to a cycle of evil that you'll all suffer from. If you're living with two mostly good roommates, on the other hand, you may be able to make the situation more manageable. "As soon as you find yourself at either end of the subgrouping phenomenon, try to intervene right away because once it begins, it's incredibly difficult to contain," says Dr. Kulic. Even mostly good roommates have the tendency to give in to subgrouping, but if you confront the dynamic head-on, you have a fighting chance of maintaining both peace in the apartment and your dignity.

Ultimately, though, the ones who really have the power to stop subgrouping are, not surprisingly, the ones in power. "It doesn't take much to be inclusive of other people," says Dr. Kulic, "and once you start a cycle of inclusion, you signal to people that you're safe to talk to and that you're willing to work things out. In any negotiation, the interchange has to begin with a demonstration of trust, and it's much more effective when the olive branch is extended by the party who is perceived as more powerful in the relationship." So if a third roommate moves into your apartment, even if you have more of an affinity for one girl, make an effort to share some "alone time" with the third as well. This can mean something as simple as going for coffee every Saturday morning, or watching the news together a couple of nights a week, even if it's just celebrity news. In addition, Dr. Lasky advises, "In a threesome situation, it's best to have house meetings on a regular basis where the agenda involves what is going well and what needs improvement. Another effective solution is to have a separate conversation with each roommate about things going on in the apartment." The point is, try your best not to exclude one roommate. It doesn't take a lot to maintain a "we're more than just roommates" relationship, even if you're just simulating one, and it'll work wonders in creating a more comfortable atmosphere in the apartment.

Things to Remember

* Two is better than three. Four or five is better than three. Any number, really, is better than three. Three girls living together is a recipe for the most extreme forms of cattiness.
* If you're set on living with two other girls, try to find ones who aren't already good friends.
* If you're set on living with two other girls, try to find ones who aren't the devil's spawn.
* Living with three girls should be done in the most egalitarian manner possible. Make all apartment decisions as a three-member team, not as a pair.
* As hard as it is, don't create solidarity with one roommate by talking negatively about the third one. And make an effort to devote "alone time" to the third, potentially left out, roommate each week.

Chapter Three
Checks and Imbalances

DO equally divide the responsibilities and the bills.
DON'T turn a blind eye to the first signs of a
roommate's financial irresponsibility.

Money issues result in the demise of all types of relationships, but roommate relationships are perhaps the most susceptible to its negative effects. Roommates have to deal with many of the same bills as married couples do, without the comfort of a shared bank account. And more important, they usually do so without the shared perspective of the ways in which money should be spent.

Nancy, a former roommate of mine, was frustratingly cheap. Here's an illustrative example of an exchange we had on numerous occasions:

"I'm running out to grab a soda. Do you want something?" she'd ask.

"No thanks," I'd say.

"Are you sure?"

"Yup."

"Nothing at all? Not even a drink?"

"Uh, okay, can you grab me a Diet Coke?"

"Ooooh. Can I get a couple of dollars then? I'm so broke right now."

No matter how much Nancy pressed, I should have just said no, no, no to having her grab me *anything* at the store, but it took a frustratingly long time

> **Myth:** Richer roommates generally don't have a problem spending more on apartment expenses than their poorer roommates. In fact, making more money means they should! **Fact:** When you're splitting the bills, you have to be conscious of unfairly hiking those bills up, whether you're the richer or poorer roommate. Things that tend to do this: pay-per-view movies, misuse of air conditioners, misuse of heat, and buying pricey specialty food and supplies.

for me to realize this. (My other roommate was quicker to learn: After getting suckered the first time, she would curtly say "nope!" before our cheap roommate had even finished her question. And if she happened to be in the room when cheap roommate was asking me if I wanted anything, she'd shoot me a look that said, "Don't do it. Do *not* do it.") These situations with the cheap roommate pissed me off so much because she turned what was a *mildly* thoughtful offer into talking me into wanting—and paying for—something I didn't even need. It was also upsetting because of the amount of money she asked for, and the fact that she *always* asked for it. I mean, let's face it, it's hard to believe someone is too broke to buy her roommate a soda when she's running to the store in Prada flats and has a $1,500 Balenciaga bag thrown over her shoulder.

She'd also refuse to contribute money to things that would have made the apartment more comfortable. For example, when my other roommate and I approached her about splitting the cost of a cleaning lady ($40 each every two weeks), she said that she'd rather spend that money on drugs, and not the medical kind. She also happened to be—surprise, surprise—the messiest of the three of us.

Choosing recreational drugs over a clean apartment was, despite her cheapness, consistent with her bouts of extravagance. She would spend $700 on a pair of designer heels or take impromptu exotic trips, and she moved into our tiny apartment with a fifty-two-inch flat-screen TV. There were times when her cheapness and extravagance overlapped, and in those instances she reverted to manipulation as a way to appease both. If, say, she happened to order a couple of bottles of wine to be delivered to the apartment, she'd jump in the shower just in time for the delivery boy to show up, leaving my other roommate and me to take care of the bill. Once she finished showering, she'd feign surprise at how fast the delivery boy had arrived, thank us, and promise to leave cash to repay us on the counter by the next morning. Then she'd pour three glasses of wine: one for herself, one for my roommate, and one for me. My other roommate and I almost never asked for any wine, and most of the time we didn't drink what she poured for us, but this was another one of her ways of "cutting costs." By forcing us to share her wine, she could justify paying us back only a portion of what the wine cost. My other roommate and I called it the well-you-had-some-too tactic.

Even then, we'd have to remind her of her debt three or four times before any money materialized. Eventually I, too, learned to never, ever ask her to pick up anything for me at the store, and if the delivery boy showed up while she was in the shower, we'd tell him he had the wrong apartment.

But her cheapness and actions had an impact on more than just our wallets. Because her behavior was underhanded and dishonest, it made us not want to open the doors to having a closer relationship with her. "Using sneaky tactics destroys any sense of trust in the relationship," says Dr. Kulic. "People will go out of their way to avoid any type of emotional intimacy with a person who acts that way."

Although dealing with a cheap and manipulative roommate is frustrating and can lead to the erosion of trust, dealing with an irresponsible one can be absolutely maddening, especially when it comes to paying bills on time. A friend of mine shared an apartment with three other girls in New York City's Gramercy Park neighborhood. One of them offered to be in charge of the power bill, meaning it was her job to collect money from the roommates each month and then pay the bill on time. Busy with their lives and other bills, none of the girls realized that six months had passed since they'd been asked to pay their portions of the bill—until one of the roommates, who worked from home, was sitting at her computer on a hot summer day when the electricity went down. *Another blackout?* she thought. *Terrorist attack?* Alarmed and sweating, she walked outside. "But when I looked around, especially when

I looked in the check-cashing/buy (and sell!) jewelry store below our apartment and saw that the lights were on, I realized the problem was specific to our apartment. I also realized I was going to have to call Con-fucking-Ed [the power company], which holds the record for having one of the worst voice recognition software systems out there." Once the roommate got through to a living, breathing representative, she found out that their bill was severely past due. Thousands of dollars past due. Desperate and shocked, she paid it immediately, on an emergency credit card. But she was furious. How had her roommate let this go? What had she done with all the warning notices from ConEd? Once the roommates confronted her, they found out that, despite her well-paying job, she had a history of letting bills go, including her own cell phone bill (which was turned off on a regular basis). Another major sign of her irresponsibility, one that the roommates had chosen to ignore, was the huge stack of unopened mail that had littered her desk since she moved in.

"We assumed that she could handle the responsibility because she made a good salary," said my friend. "In fact, she made quite a bit more than any of us. But if she couldn't even take care of her own bills, how was she supposed to take care of one that involved four people?" My friend learned the hard way that a steady income does not a good roommate make. Dr. Kulic warns, "It's important to take personalities into account: Careless people tend to be careless with everything."

Once everything was out in the open, the roommates admitted to being neglectful by not inquiring about the bill each month. They learned that while the careless roommate clearly wasn't the best person to be in charge of such an important bill, they had only enabled her by sticking their heads in the sand. The embarrassment the irresponsible roommate openly felt for what she'd done helped the other roommates forgive her, but they were much more careful with all the apartment bills from that point forward. To prevent even getting to the point they did, Dr. Pass suggests that a contract be drafted and signed by all roommates before moving in together: "This should be a binding agreement with expectations and contingencies." You see, people are more likely to fulfill their responsibilities if a contract exists—a contract they themselves were a part of creating. Dr. Kulic adds, "The best plan of action in a shared-bills situation is to have a regular check-in time during which everyone deals with the status of the bills and is forced to be accountable on a regular basis."

While it angered and shocked the Gramercy Park girls that their roommate was so irresponsible with financial matters, at least they knew she wasn't a con artist. Perhaps flighty and immature, but not shady. Unfortunately, that wasn't the case for Pia, a friend of mine who lived with two girls in Baltimore. One of the stipulations of their lease was that rather than turn in three separate checks every month, they only turn in one check for the full amount. This responsibility—turning in the rent check every month—was happily, excitedly even, taken on by Dana, one of the roommates. Pia and her other roommate, Lucy, didn't think it was strange that Dana jumped at the opportunity to be in charge of this. They thought Dana, who was the only one with a car, volunteered because it was easier for her to make trips to the bank to deposit the roommates' individual checks.

"Lucy and I always gave Dana our checks on time," said Pia. "Every month we made sure we gave them to her five days before rent was due so that they would clear by the time Dana wrote the big check to our landlord."

For months, this routine worked perfectly. Then Pia received an angry call from her father, who was a guarantor on the lease. "Our landlord had called him to inform him that we were $11,000 past due on our rent," said Pia. "Rather than using our money to pay the rent, Dana was stealing it." After that, things that had appeared faintly fishy in the apartment suddenly started to make sense. "Dana was always cooking these huge five-course dinners for herself," said Pia. "Not only would she not offer Lucy and me any of the food she cooked, she'd specifically ask that we not touch her leftovers. Then they'd sit in the fridge for two days before getting thrown out." Meanwhile, Pia and Lucy, who, like Dana, were earning entry-level salaries, were living on cheap food, like pasta and butter, and peanut butter on saltines. "What we eventually found out was that Dana was dining on our dime," said Pia. Not coincidentally, she had also put herself in charge of paying the utilities. "She'd keep the bills in a lock box, so we never saw them. Instead, she'd post the amount we owed on a dry erase board every month. Yes, we should've questioned the $250 we paid her in cash each month, but we didn't."

Duplicitous Dana also managed to intercept every single one of the eviction notices that had been sent to the apartment. "She told the landlord that Lucy and I weren't paying her," Pia told me, "so she could only afford to pay him $250 to $650 per month. We had no idea what was happening behind our backs. She made the landlord think we were the ones conning her."

After the phone call from Pia's dad, Lucy and Pia kicked "that crazy bitch" out of their apartment. Eventually, a family member of Dana's was contacted, and they were able to get almost all their money back. But it was time and energy that Pia and Lucy would rather have spent doing other stuff, like, say, spreading peanut butter on saltines while searching for a new roommate.

There's not too much one can do to protect oneself against a con artist. If someone is set on conning you, she will probably be able to get away with it, at least for a little while, but there are some precautions you can take to avoid getting conned the way Lucy and Pia were. Asking to see the ConEd bill every month before they paid their portions would have helped. Pia and Lucy also should have called or e-mailed their landlord within the first month, asking him to notify them by phone or e-mail if their rent was ever late. The point is, don't ever relinquish all responsibility of any communal bill. It's fine to designate the responsibility of various bills to each roommate, but that doesn't mean you shouldn't check up on the status of those bills periodically. To avoid situations like this, Dr. Lasky advises doing something similar to what Dr. Kulic suggests: Hold regular financial meetings. "They're a wonderful ritual that I've used successfully with patients who are roommates," she says. "I like to structure it as a weekly meeting in the beginning in which all bills are opened and each person writes down their share of the costs simultaneously. Discussions about whether or not the amounts spent on each item seem reasonable can be introduced and usually feel appropriate during this time. As time goes by, you may be able to switch to every-other-week meetings or even once-a-month meetings." While this is always a great tactic, even before anything bad happens in normal, healthy roommate situations, it'll also prevent girls like Dana from getting away with conning you.

The irresponsible roommate who forgot to pay her apartment's ConEd bill wasn't looking to scam her roommates the way Dana was; she was just bad at handling money. Lucky for my friends, she had the money to pay them back immediately. But what happens when a roommate doesn't have the money? What happens when she's living beyond her means and is too embarrassed to admit it? My friend Susan was living in Atlanta when she discovered the ramifications of living with a financially delusional roommate. "I was looking for someone to split the rent with me on this great house I found," said Susan. "So I called my college friend Ruthie, who I knew was desperate for a new living situation." Ruthie moved in right away, and for the first three months, things went smoothly. "Then," said Susan, "the rent check she wrote me bounced." Ruthie assured Susan that it was a bank error and had nothing to do with insufficient funds in her account. Susan, not knowing better, believed her. "This girl worked at a financial institution," Susan said. "I thought, surely she must be good at managing her money." Not the case: The check Ruthie wrote Susan to cover the bounced check also bounced. Now Susan's antennae were up, and she started to investigate. "I ended up learning through mutual friends that Ruthie was only making $1,200 a month. Our rent was $700 a month, per person. No wonder her checks were bouncing!"

At this point Susan should've confronted Ruthie. Even though they were friends, she could've nipped things in the bud by telling her that although she wanted to maintain their friendship, she couldn't afford to live with someone whose checks kept bouncing. Susan knew how much Ruthie made for a living, so the chances of things improving, unless she hit the lottery, were slim. The best decision Susan could've made? To find another roommate. Perhaps this would've strained their friendship temporarily, but by continuing to live with Ruthie, it put a strain on their friendship permanently. "I felt bad kicking her out because she was a friend," Susan admitted. So what happened? Susan ended up paying the rent for the both of them until their lease was up. "I spent $5,000 of my own savings to support the both of us." Ruthie would give Susan money when she could ("a few hundred dollars now and then"), but it wasn't nearly enough. "To make matters worse," said Susan, "for three weeks she told me that her car was in the shop, so I gave her rides everywhere—to work, to the store, to the dentist. Then I found out, it had been repoed!" Even when Susan confronted Ruthie about her money situation, Ruthie continued to lie and say the money was coming. She was simply too embarrassed to admit that she couldn't afford the lifestyle she was living. "Charity is one thing; being taken advantage of is another," says Dr. Kulic. "People [like Susan] often feel that they need to do everything they can to 'save' their friend. Guilt is a very powerful motivator." In Ruthie's mind, she probably believed that she'd be able to pay Susan back, that money would eventually come to her. But it never did. "It was wrong of Ruthie to put Susan in a position like this in the first place," insists Dr. Kulic. "It was unfair for Ruthie to expect Susan to support her, and she clearly had no qualms about abusing Susan's goodwill. It might have been nice for Susan to extend Ruthie a month to find somewhere else to live (by saying something like, 'I'll hook you up this month, but I can't afford to do this moving forward'), but she really wound up just enabling Ruthie to continue abusing her."

"After our lease was up, we didn't talk for a few months," Susan said. "She finally called me, and I told her everything I had ever felt about the situation. Now we're on much better terms, but to be honest, after what happened, she's never going to be one of my favorite people." If Ruthie had been honest about her money situation, she would've been able to salvage a friendship, which is ultimately more important than living in a townhouse that you can't afford.

Inevitably, at some point in a girl's roommate career, she will live with a person who makes more or less money than she does. Living with a richer roommate who is generous and understanding can be very helpful when you're struggling to make ends meet, but you should never *expect* her to pay your way. I, for example, lived with a roommate at a point in my life when I made barely enough to survive each month. She, on the other hand, made enough to comfortably pay the full rent herself if she wanted to. Having a roommate was her way of *saving* money, but it wasn't a necessity for her. While I never asked for big loans, she was, thankfully, incredibly tolerant and laid-back, so on months when I couldn't come up with my share of the rent on the day it was due, she would cover me for a couple of weeks or so. I always ended up paying her back, but I wouldn't have been able to stay living in New York at that time with the job I had if she hadn't provided this cushion for me.

I was fortunate to live with a richer roommate who was generous with her money, but other girls aren't so lucky. One of my friends lived with a roommate who made more money than she did but wasn't as generous as my former roommate had been. To make matters worse, my friend's roommate also spent beyond even her own means. "She had very, very expensive taste, which often exceeded her own salary," my friend explained. "Everything she bought—food, wine, champagne,

candles—was top of the line. It was hard to keep up with her."
My friend's roommate didn't *force* her to buy the same stuff she
did, but if you're used to buying $3.99 vanilla-scented candles
from CVS, and your roommate only buys $50 candles from an
exclusive boutique, you're less inclined to burn your cheap
candles in the apartment. "I constantly felt like a pauper," my
friend said. "My Finesse shampoo looked even cheaper next
to her Bumble and Bumble conditioner, and my frozen Ellio's
pizzas seemed ridiculous sitting next to her Häagen-Dazs ice
cream. We were on totally different pages financially." If my
friend ever did order food to be delivered to the apartment,
which was rare, she usually called the cheap Thai place around
the corner from her. Occasionally, my friend's roommate would
ask her if she wanted to order takeout together. "I made the
mistake of agreeing to order takeout with her only a couple of
times, and I totally regretted it afterward. I was embarrassed
to say the sushi place she ordered from was too expensive for
me, so I'd end up having to pay $30 for my portion of dinner.
Sometimes $30 was all I had to spend on food for the whole
week!" My friend's roommate's expensive taste made it hard
for my friend to not feel self-conscious, and it was difficult for
them to do anything together, even order food or go grocery
shopping, because of their vastly different financial situations
and views. This also precluded them from ever getting close as
roommates or friends.

Eventually, my friend moved out. The next girl she lived
with had a lifestyle similar to hers and was much more frugal

than the prior roommate. "It made things so much easier and more comfortable. It also ended up being more economical for me because I didn't feel pressured into buying stuff I couldn't afford, like lobster rolls from Nobu."

Things to Remember

* If you find yourself living with a cheap roommate, don't ever lend or borrow money. You'll have to spend too much time and energy fighting to get paid back, or they'll make you feel like you owe them your firstborn child because they spotted you $10 once.
* Even if one roommate is assigned the responsibility of a bill, don't relinquish all responsibility of the bill yourself. Inquire about the bills' status each month.
* Set up—and stick to—all monthly meetings having to do with the finances of the apartment, even if the meetings only last for five or ten minutes.
* Make it a point to pay apartment bills before personal bills each month.
* Try to find a roommate whose taste and salary are somewhat similar to yours. It can be hard to keep up with a roommate's expensive taste if you're living on an entry-level salary and she's not.

Chapter Four

Idiosyncrasies or Idiosyncrazies?

DO your best to find out about a person's
character before moving in with her.
DON'T continue to live with a roommate who reveals
that she doesn't have a normal sense of reality.

"I've lived with the *craziest* girls," one of my friends said over drinks recently.

"You couldn't have," my other friend said, laughing. "Because *I've* ended up sharing apartments with all of them."

And here I thought I was the preeminent crazy roommate magnet.

Unfortunately, the crazy girls I've lived with were not funny crazy or you're-so-crazy crazy. They were just plain scary crazy. The craziest roommate I had was a girl I found on Craigslist.[2] It was partly my fault for rushing into something

[2]Craigslist has become such a regular part of our vernacular and day-to-day lives that we act as if it's more secure than it really is. And although it can be a relatively safe place to find relatively sane roommates, among other things, it's also important

without doing a sufficient amount of research on the person I'd be sharing a tiny Chelsea apartment with, but I never could've anticipated this girl's level of insanity.

Just for fun, let's call her Sunshine, even though that's the opposite of what she was. Many of Sunshine's comments and musings on life struck me as odd from the minute I met her, but I gave her the benefit of the doubt and excused them as idiosyncrasies rather than what they really were: idiosyncrazies. Her Craigslist posting said she was seeking a "nice, clean, sane" roommate, and I was in a crunch to find a new place to live. *If those are her requirements, I thought, then she must also be nice, clean, and sane. Perfect.* When we first met at her apartment, I didn't ask her too many questions or inquire about her personal life much. I realize now that I overlooked a few warning signs and neglected to delve too deeply behind her normal-seeming facade because I didn't want to deal with the fact that she might be a freak or a less-than-ideal roommate. She, on the other hand, fired a barrage of questions at me, questions more suitable for a

> **Myth:** *Single White Female* is just a movie. People that crazy don't actually exist.
> **Fact:** People that crazy do exist and they put postings seeking roommates up on the Internet all the time.

to be wary of this "centralized network of online communities," since it can attract a shitload of crazies who would like very much to be your roommate. Remember this: Simply because someone advertises that they're looking to live with a "normal, nice, sane" person does not mean that they themselves are normal, nice, and sane. Don't ever turn off your crazy detector, no matter how desperate you are for a roommate or a place to live.

potential mate: What time do you like to eat dinner? Where do you see yourself in ten years? When was the last time you had a boyfriend? What type of guys do you like? What type of music do you listen to? What's your sign? Do you consider yourself spiritual? If I hadn't turned my crazy detector off, her questions would've struck me as a bit odd. The way she asked them—intensely and sternly—as her cat creepily rubbed up against her leg should've made me feel like I was being interviewed by Gargamel and Azrael, the Smurfs' nemesis and his cat. Also, I wasn't filling out a profile on Match.com; why the hell did she care what my "type" was, or what time I ate dinner? But again, since I was desperate, I just went along with it.

There's nothing wrong with asking questions, mind you. It's encouraged, in fact, but just as it's important to pay attention to a potential roommate's answers to your questions, it's equally important to pay attention to the type of questions she asks you. Her questions, like her answers, may reveal that she's looking for more than just a roommate—a best friend, perhaps, or maybe even a partner. And the interview process should be more than just a question-and-answer session; it should be about getting to know each other. The more personal questions should come up organically, as you're hanging out. "You need to spend time together before you move in together," insists Dr. Pass. "Go to dinner and talk. Living together is a huge commitment, and people can underestimate that in nonromantic situations." You're not marrying your roommate and you don't have to "play house" with each other, but you do have to make some serious commitments to each other, ones that require you to be on the same page, mentally. If you approach a roommate situation as if it were a marriage (meaning that you take the commitment seriously and not that you act like husband and wife), you're bound to be a lot more selective about who you move in with. Dr. Pass says, "Living together is *like* a marriage, which means you need to date each other first." So while it's okay to ask questions (and by *ask*, I don't mean fire them at your potential roommate), don't depend on them to reveal who your potential roommate really is, unless you're spending quality time together while you're asking those questions. "Only asking specific questions isn't always the best route because people can lie," Dr. Pass says. Which is what my Craigslist roommate did when she claimed to be sane. (Although I guess she wasn't technically lying since *she* considered herself to be sane.)

Getting back to Sunshine's apartment, "tiny" probably isn't the best way to describe it. As a whole, it wasn't that small. In fact, it was bigger than the apartment I was moving out of; what was positively claustrophobia inducing and smaller than any area I'd ever seen a human live in for an extended period of time was my bedroom. Here's what I could fit in it: a twin bed, which isn't the type of purchase an adult is ever proud to make (When I ordered it over the phone, the Sleepy's representative, frustrated with my mumbling, finally said, "Honey, you're gonna have to speak up. Did you say *twin*?"), a small

TV, and a bookshelf that had to be turned on its side (it then functioned as a place to store my books, my underwear, and a couple of picture frames). The rent was steep ($1,000 a month to sleep in what was essentially a walk-in closet), but I figured it was worth it since the apartment was otherwise a decent size. Again, I was in a crunch, and I was desperate; at this point, I probably could've justified renting a tent on a sidewalk somewhere as long as it had some semblance of a door. I made myself believe that she was the right roommate and this was the right apartment, which means I should never, ever trust myself to make major decisions when I'm desperate.

Bad stuff started happening right off the bat. The day I was supposed to move in, which had been mutually agreed on during one of our "introductory meetings" (I even saw her write the date down in her Trapper Keeper–like planner), she was nowhere to be found. I didn't have keys yet, so I was stuck outside the apartment with a van full of stuff and two friends who had a limited amount of time to help me move. After calling her for hours, I finally parked the van on the street and retreated to a friend's house. She didn't show up or return my calls for another two days. "I must've gotten the date confused!" she blithely chirped when I finally got in touch with her. And *I* must've gone temporarily color-blind, because bright red flags were popping up all over the place and I still moved in.

The third night of the first week I lived with Sunshine, I was woken up at 2:00 a.m. by her loud and out-of-tune singing. With a pillow over my head, I forced myself back to sleep, but I soon learned that she did this regularly. That is, put on a melancholy CD late at night and then loudly, drunkenly, and very badly—like, I'm not kidding, a hyena in heat—sing herself to sleep until the neighbors from the adjacent building would take turns screaming, "Shut the hell up!" I was horrified and embarrassed, but I continued to justify her behavior: "Well, I do some crazy stuff too when I'm drunk," I tried to tell myself. The weirdest part about it was that she'd never address it the next day, and neither would I, but we both knew the other one knew what had occurred the night before. By the third week, I ran out of excuses for her. "Maybe she's just lonely?" I asked my friends, grasping for an explanation as to why she would share almost all her meals with her cat, who would eat right off her plate, sometimes even off her fork.

"Yeah, shocking nobody wants to be around her," they'd say while rolling their eyes.

When I finally admitted to myself that I was living with a crazy person, I still didn't leave. It's not that I'm a masochist, really; I'm just lazy. Which was a supremely stupid reason to stay, considering the fact that it takes way more energy to live with a crazy person than it does to go out and find another place to live. "There are a lot of reasons why people stay in very bad situations," says Dr. Kulic. "And a lot of it has to do with investment, not just financial. Consider, for example, why you might stay with a really bad boyfriend for any period of time—did you think maybe you could help him through it, that you could make him better? Also, people are heavily invested in their places, and they don't want to give up their spaces just because their roommates are crazy." Moving, as anyone who lives in a major city knows, is expensive and exhausting, and I was determined to stick it out and find a way to make my living situation bearable.

So I stayed, and things only got worse. For example, dinnertime in the apartment became particularly difficult, simply because she found it offensive that I didn't want to sit down, eat, and take turns discussing our days together. When I say she found it offensive, I mean she would get overtly mad at me, slamming doors, plates, and drawers for the remainder of the night. I was able to escape some of these dinners by coming up with excuses for why I'd be home late (as if, like a bad mate, I was cheating on her) until she reached the pinnacle of desperation.

"Hey, do you like pork chops?" she asked me one day in passing.

"I guess," I answered tentatively, not asking "why" for fear that she'd conspiratorially ask if, like her, I'd noticed that most of them were shaped like cows. What I hadn't realized was that by answering "sure" I'd somehow agreed to sit down to a pork chop dinner with her, something that became apparent when I walked into the apartment that evening to find a table complete with two place settings and a fully cooked meal, which is almost impossible to get out of, especially when the only people present are you and the chef. Who knew that an ostensibly innocent question like

"Do you like pork chops?" could be used as entrapment?

What was most frustrating about being kidnapped for dinner was that, after we finished, she had the nerve to ask me for money. "I paid about $30 for everything, so it's probably fair if you give me $10–$15." Crazy people do that a lot, I've noticed: try to force you into doing something you don't want to do, then trick you into doing it, and finally, once you're reluctantly participating, make it seem like they're doing you a huge favor. (It's a 101 class they must teach at crazy school, and students can't graduate without it.) From that point forward, I admitted to liking almost no food, unless it was something that could be eaten on the run, like a granola bar or string cheese.

In a matter of two months, I went from ignoring the signs, to justifying her nutty behavior, to living with her nutty behavior, to becoming terrified of her. To illustrate how bad things finally got, here's the conversation that was the catalyst to my moving out:

Sunshine: My ex-boyfriend has been so annoying lately.
Me: Really? Why?
*Sunshine: He's just been coming around a lot, showing up at
    the apartment, trying to have sex with me. He's been really
    sexually aggressive.*
Me: Wait, I thought you told me that he's traveling in India.
*Sunshine: Yeah, he is. It's his energy that's been coming
    around, not his physical body, which can be a lot more
    powerful. His energy actually raped me while I was lying*

in bed the other night. It was really traumatic.
Me: Oh. God. What a horrible nightmare.
Sunshine: No. It wasn't a nightmare. **His energy raped me.**
Remind me to burn some sage later.

And then it hit me like a frying pan: I simply couldn't stay in the apartment for one more minute. She was capable of accusing the spirit of her still-living ex-boyfriend (an ex-boyfriend who had broken up with her!) of brutally raping her in the middle of the night, so what would she eventually accuse me of? She was also completely unaware of how crazy she sounded. Some people are at least semiaware that their views are a tad eccentric. Not Sunshine. If anything, she acted like she was the sane one and I was the one who needed help.

"Energy is a very powerful thing, Amy," she said to me after her rape claim. "It doesn't always *stay with the body*." She might as well have just said, "Duh."

She also chastised me when I "inappropriately" handled mundane things. One time, for example, I was heating up food in the microwave and I opened the door without pressing the stop button first.

"Oh my God, what are you doing?" she asked, covering her face with her hands.

"What?"

"Amy, Amy, Amy, don't you know that you're exposing yourself to harmful radiation when you open the door like that?"

"No. How much radiation could I really be getting exposed to?"

"It's very, very bad for you. I can't believe you don't know that," she said, and then tsk-tsk'd her way out of the kitchen.

The way she looked at me, with a mix of pity and disbelief, made me want to punch her in the head. How did someone as crazy as she was become so self-righteous and condescending? "A person like this thinks that everything is about them," says Dr. Lewis. "They're exquisitely selfish, and they will not consider your feelings at all." Sunshine didn't care that she startled me out of sleep with her singing on a weekly basis, or how uncomfortable being forced into dinner with her made me. Everything was about her and her crazy needs.

Later that week I told her I was leaving. The truth was, I was putting my stuff in storage and staying with a friend until I found another place to live. This is what I told her: "Something happened, and I can't afford to pay $1,000 a month to live here anymore. I'm sorry." Which wasn't a *total* lie: Something had happened (she had irreversibly freaked me out), and I couldn't afford to stay (my sanity and safety were at stake).

"Oh my God," she said, shocked, as most crazy people are when you let them know you want out of their craziness. "Well, what about if I only charge you $500?"

At that point she could have offered to let me stay there for free and I would've said no, but her response pissed me off more than anything she had done in the past two months because if she could afford to charge me only $500 for the room, then she had clearly been overcharging me since I moved in. Sadly, this is what it comes down to: I had been overpaying to get tortured.

"For that price, I'm sure you'll have no problem finding someone to take over the room," I finally said, seething.

My move-out was swift and clean, with no big fights or tantrums on her part, but it certainly wasn't comfortable. She stayed out of my way—ignored me, really—and when I was done, I left the keys on the kitchen counter. A couple of weeks later, she e-mailed me in an attempt to collect money I owed her for a phone bill. It was a paltry amount—maybe $20—and because I was still seething from the realization that she'd overcharged me for my room, I chose to ignore her. She, though, still seemed to be upset that I'd left her, so she e-mailed me constantly, sometimes multiple times a day, until finally I relented and sent her a check. After that, I didn't hear from her, but about a year later, I saw her on the street. We made eye contact, and I slowed down as we passed each other, but as I did so the scary flashbacks—uncomfortable pork chop dinners and drunken late-night sing-alongs—popped into my head, so rather than make small talk, I looked away, picked up the pace, and just kept moving.

Unfortunately, that wasn't my only stop on the crazy roommate train. I once lived with a girl who revealed her craziness through her overbearing generosity. Her name was Suzie, but she insisted on being called "Suze." Not Sue, not Susan. Suze. It was a name my other roommate and I refused to call her, no

matter how many times she corrected us. Why? Because, as
any sane person knows, it's simply not okay to give yourself
your own nickname, and then insist on other people using it.

What I'd initially thought was Suzie's sweet inclination to
share turned out to be a weird disorder. She would do things
like consistently offer me Zoloft as if it were a recreational drug
and not a prescribed antidepressant. Aside from the fact that
Zoloft, unlike some pharmaceuticals, isn't even a fun drug, if
she had enough to spare, she couldn't have been taking the
medication properly. When I said no to the Zoloft, she'd offer
me a caffeine pill. When I said no to the caffeine pill, she'd
offer me a Vitamin B supplement. And on the occasions when
she did happen to be using real recreational drugs, she'd turn
into a full-blown pusher.

"You want some coke?" she'd ask.

"No, thanks," I'd say.

"Here, just a little," she'd implore.

"No, really. I don't want any."

This would go on for some time, until I would get annoyed
enough to snap at her. Once I snapped, she'd give me this
wounded look she'd come to perfect, as if to say, "Okaaay,
geez, sorry, I was just trying to be nice." Suzie's craziness
prevented her from understanding that if a person in her late
twenties wants to do drugs, she'll usually do them, especially
if they're being offered for free. With drugs, no almost always
means no. It's not like a piece of chocolate cake, where an
"Oh, c'mon, one bite won't hurt" can convince us to indulge.

(At this age we're no longer living in D.A.R.E. territory. Either we've already developed a drug habit—in which case we don't need to be persuaded to do them—sworn them off, or designated certain times for doing them, and usually 7:00 p.m. on a Monday night isn't one of those times.) But she didn't separate things like chocolate cake from drugs. In her mind dessert and drugs were essentially the same: treats you should share with people.

She didn't adhere to basic societal norms. If you're going to do drugs, particularly a drug like cocaine, you at least *try* to be discreet about it. Sure, maybe everyone suspects you're doing it, but that's not the point. If you're the only one doing it, you don't just lay it out on the table, like you would a cheese plate.

Cigarettes were also pushed on us—again, something else that can't really be forced on people, unless they've already developed a habit. My roommate and I would smoke socially, as did some of the friends we invited over. Suzie, I think, tried to smoke socially, but didn't enjoy it. If she saw a bunch of us drinking and some of us smoking in the living room, she'd immediately join in, equipped with her own pack of cigarettes. ("So expensive these days!" she'd exclaim, shaking her head.) Then she'd position herself in the middle of the group and light cigarette after cigarette, taking only one short drag and then passing it off to whoever was closest to her, even if they hadn't asked for it, even if they didn't smoke, ever. "Here," she'd say to the person next to her.

"Oh, no. I don't smoke," the victim would say, recoiling.

"No, here," she'd insist, with a saintlike tilt of the head.

"No, really. I don't smoke."

Flustered and annoyed, and trying to prevent getting burned, the victim would usually end up taking the lit cigarette and then putting it out, but it bothered guests to the point where some of them would get up and leave.

She also pushed food, particularly baked goods (and, no, shockingly not the kind with drugs in them). On the surface, food seems like a normal thing to share, but with her it wasn't. I'm convinced she didn't even enjoy baking and did it simply to appease her sharing disorder. She'd buy boxes and boxes of cake and muffin mix and then maniacally bake for, say, an entire Saturday.

I was awakened many weekend mornings to the sound of knocking at my bedroom door. "Would you prefer blueberry or banana muffins?" Suzie would ask, as if this were the most normal thing in the world.

"Uh . . . I don't know, either one?" I'd mumble.

"Okay, I'll just make both then!"

And off she went into a baking frenzy, setting the smoke alarm off at regular intervals throughout the day. Anyone could see that it wasn't the act of baking that did it for her. She didn't seem to give a shit about how they came out, or whether or not they were melt-in-your-mouth soft or rock hard, which means they were *always* rock hard. People who genuinely enjoy baking try out different recipes, carefully mix ingredients together, check on their cookies or muffins once they're in the oven, and taste them before offering them to others. She didn't do any of these things. She bought the same old boxes of Duncan Hines cake and muffin mix, messily threw the ingredients into a bowl, plopped gooey balls of the mix onto a pan, shoved them in the oven, and then forgot about them. Never, in the entire time I lived with her, did I ever see her eat one bite of the things she baked, but they were relentlessly pushed on me and any other person who happened to walk through our front door. (Incidentally, if I'm going to eat a high-calorie food, like a cookie, it's going to be soft and delicious and not have the consistency of a hockey puck.) She did the same thing with popcorn. Almost every night before she went to bed, she'd ask, "Do you guys want some popcorn?"

"No, thanks," my roommate and I would mumble from the couch.

"Okay, well, I'll just make it, and you guys can eat what you want." It didn't matter what we said, or how we answered. Even if one of us had said, "Suzie, I'm so allergic to popcorn, my throat will close up and I'll die if I eat it," she probably still would've offered it to us.

After witnessing this routine a number of times, a friend finally said, "Huh. Most people brush their teeth before going to bed; Suzie makes popcorn."

I know it seems a bit harsh to call someone crazy because they like to share their stuff more than most, but she wasn't sharing out of the goodness of her heart. It was something else entirely. Her need to share created more work for my other roommate and me, whether it was airing out the apartment after she'd burnt yet another batch of cookies or dealing with the embarrassment of her indiscretion with drugs. (An old high school friend I hadn't seen in five years stopped by for a drink on a weeknight once and Suzie pulled out a plate of drugs. "Hi! I'm Suze. Want some?" she casually asked her. There was an uncomfortably long pause and then my friend politely said, "Oh. No, thanks." But it was apparent that she was horrified. In fact, I think it took her so long to respond because it took a while for her to register exactly what it was that was being offered to her.)

I'm sure if a neurosurgeon took an X-ray of Suzie's brain, there'd be a part that showed more or less activity in the "sharing" section than what's normal, but like many neuroses, there was no logical reason for her need to share in the manner she did. One can speculate that she hoped to get something out of it, maybe that people would like her more if she always had something to offer them. One might also wonder if she was trying to fatten us up for slaughter, like in "Hansel and Gretel" (or *Silence of the Lambs*). But there's often no good reason for the crazy things crazy people do. The fact of the matter is that certain people simply aren't fit to live with others, especially when they're offering up their drugs (including their antidepressants) as if they were Gummi Bears.

My other roommate and I put up with Suzie for more than a year, a mistake on our parts because we had to endure constant craziness in the apartment, to the point where we started to feel crazy ourselves. (My friend Jen describes the phenomenon like this: "It's like when you're having a conversation with a person who has an accent and then you start talking like them. Same thing.") Although we didn't mimic her behavior, in order to deal with her, we had to occasionally think the way she thought: If my roommate and I both happened to be going away for the weekend, we'd have to sit down and think, "What's Suzie gonna do in the apartment all by herself?"

"It's very easy to become enmeshed in the world of thought of someone who's not well," says Dr. Kulic. "Because you need to worry about your own well-being as well as the condition of your belongings, you'll find yourself thinking like the enemy, but it's unhealthy to let someone stress you out to the point where you start suffering symptomatically because of it."

People who have vacation homes in Florida have to board up their houses during hurricane season; we had to protect our apartment from another kind of impending disaster, but one that was potentially as dangerous. "Lock bedroom doors, hide laptops, and lie about return date," we'd say in unison as we hung out in each other's rooms and prepared to leave for the weekend. We'd take turns lying about which one of us was coming back a day earlier than we actually were so that she couldn't throw any major weekend-long "sharing" parties. You see, as much as living with a crazy person can be damaging to our mental health and to our relationships, they're also a huge liability. Who wants to go away for the weekend and spend the whole time worrying about her apartment burning down because her roommate is too crazy to remember to take muffins out of the oven?

Chicago-based Linda can relate to dealing with crazy roommate behavior: She was in a constant state of frustration after the first couple of months of living with Norah, who she moved in with despite her intuition and against her friends' warnings. "Friends of mine knew *of her* in college, and they used to call her 'Weeping Willow' because she was always crying about something," said Linda. "Stupidly, I moved in with her anyway." In the beginning Norah and Linda had the "normal roommate arguments," but then the true Norah began to manifest herself when she started dating a guy who went by the nickname Meatpie. "He was overweight, greasy, and had piercings and a really bad fashion sense," Linda said. "He also liked to walk around in only a bath towel, and he'd leave piles of his dirty dishes in the sink for me to clean up." Meatpie was a problem, yes, but it was the way in which Norah dealt with Linda's issues with Meatpie that was the real problem. "When I expressed to her that it made me uncomfortable when Meatpie walked around in only a towel, she just rolled her eyes and told me to grow up."

Neither Norah nor Meatpie had jobs (Norah was attending graduate school "sometimes" and nobody knew what Meatpie did, besides eat a lot), so they would take off for days at a time to go to music festivals, leaving a mess and Norah's unfriendly dog behind. "I would come home from work to dog shit everywhere, and Norah was nowhere to be found. It was disgusting," Linda said. "When I'd complain to Norah about her leaving the dog in my care, she said I didn't have to take care of him, that dogs could be left alone for a couple of days at a time."

Things continued to worsen over the months, with Linda complaining and Norah getting pissed off at her complaints, so in an attempt to defuse the tension, Linda tried to propose an amicable sit-down: "I knocked on her bedroom door one night, and when she opened it, I told her that we needed to talk."

"No," Norah said flatly.

"Why?" Linda asked, shocked.

"None of your business," she shot back, and then slammed the door in Linda's face.

By this point Norah had gotten a part-time job as a student teacher, which caused her to become even more irritable—not unusual when a person gets her first real job at age twenty-six. The morning after Linda's failed attempt at a peace talk, Linda was getting ready for work, blow-drying her hair in the bathroom. Norah started banging on the door, yelling that Linda was going to make her late. When Linda told her she'd be done in a few minutes, Norah completely lost it, started screaming, and then kicked the door in. Norah then yanked the blow-dryer plug out of the socket and started yelling.

"You're going to make me laaaate," Norah cried. "I have an obligation to the children!"

Linda, scared and in shock at this point, walked back

into her bedroom and continued getting dressed for work, but within a few minutes, Norah barged in with a bowl of water and threw it on her. "If you're going to make me late, I'm going to make you late!" Norah screamed.

"It took everything I had in me not to punch her," Linda said, "but I needed to get to work, and who knew what else she was capable of?" Norah, on the other hand, was on an unstoppable rampage. After Linda dried herself off and finished getting dressed, she headed for the front door. Unfortunately, she had to pass by the kitchen on her way out. Perched on top of one of the countertops was Norah—a sight that was scarily reminiscent of Rick Moranis in *Ghostbusters* when he morphs into the Keymaster. "She had a big bowl of water, and she started cursing and screaming and then threw the water on me, this time totally drenching me. I just stood there, in shock, for a few seconds, wiped the water out of my eyes, walked back into my room, changed, pulled my hair back, and left. I was pissed, shaking, and scared. But at least I wasn't late for work, which is what she wanted."

Linda was stuck in a lease with Norah for another five months following the incident, so they had to come up with a schedule that didn't allow them to ever be in the apartment at the same time—a frustrating and unfair arrangement for Linda because, after all, what the hell had she done to deserve this? "People [like Norah]," says Dr. Lewis, "personalize everything. They're lacking in empathy while being oversensitive at the same time." In other words, Norah didn't have the ability to see how she was affecting Linda's life, but overinterpreted everything Linda did to her, even if it was harmless, which is a dangerous combination. I prefer to call these people crazy, but Dr. Lewis has a more politically correct way of describing them: "Their connection to reality is loose."

Just as I never could have anticipated the insanity of Sunshine or Suzie, Linda could not have predicted how badly things would turn out between her and Norah. But Linda and I both ignored our instincts from the very beginning, instincts that told us something was off with these girls, instincts that could've saved us from a lot of pain and suffering.

And while these stories prove that paying attention to your instincts is of the utmost importance when first meeting a potential roommate, there are sociopaths and pathological liars out there who are highly adept at making very good first impressions. These are extreme examples, but think Scott Peterson, or Patrick Bateman in *American Psycho*,[3] only in

[3] This 2000 film, based on the Bret Easton Ellis novel, is about a smokin' hot Wall Street guy (Christian Bale) who leads a double life: one that includes the typical douche bag stuff: cheating on his girlfriend (Reese Witherspoon), hitting on his secretary (Chloë Sevigny), blowing lines in dirty bathroom stalls—all while wearing perfectly tailored Armani suits. In his other life, he brutally murders colleagues, strangers, and hookers whenever the hell he feels like it. None of the people in his "normal" life (Reese and Chloe, for example) have any idea who he really is. Why? Because he effortlessly switches from one life to the next, just like plenty of real-life sociopaths. Okay, it's very unlikely that you'll end up living with the next American Psycho, but there are degrees of insanity, and the beauty of crazy people is that they can embrace and exhibit all different types and levels of craziness. They're all around us, especially in major cities. They'll fool you into thinking they're successful, put-together, and generally great. The second you sense that you're living with one, don't beat yourself up over having been tricked by them; just find another place to live immediately, and never, ever leave a forwarding address.

female form. Your instincts, no matter how good they are, still may not be as good as your potential roommate is at tricking you into thinking she's normal.

Tara, a graphic artist living in Seattle, fell under the spell of one of these pathological liars. The girl she moved in with, Betsey, seemed cool and fun and easygoing at first. In fact, based on their initial meetings, Tara felt like she had hit the roommate jackpot with Betsey, who claimed to be a music producer. Tara thought her new roommate was responsible, smart, and ambitious, someone to look up to. Shortly after they moved in together, though, Tara found out Betsey wasn't really who she thought she was. "First of all, she worked in retail, not the music industry. Also, there were always these guys flying into Seattle to see her, from all over the place—Los Angeles, Texas, Ohio, everywhere. Betsey just told me they were old high school friends, but when I'd strike up a conversation with these guys, they'd tell me this was the first time they'd met her. All they knew was that she had 'a great job in the music industry as a record producer,' which, of course, she didn't. Who knew what else she was telling them. Basically, she was meeting them on the Internet and then lying to me about how she knew them." Over time, the lies proliferated, and Tara realized that Betsey was constantly lying in an attempt to trump other people's stories. "At one point, I had a yeast infection—one of those things girls talk to each other about," said Tara. "When it came up in conversation, she told me that she had suffered from such a severe one once that the hospital had to put her in a bubble. A bubble! She even went so far as to say that her mother had to put on a full plastic suit just to visit her. All because of a yeast infection, okay?" The only thing worse than being known for having the World's Worst Yeast Infection is being known for *lying* about having the World's Worst Yeast Infection.

Tara didn't kick Betsey out or move out herself once she realized that Betsey was a pathological liar. She didn't see Betsey as dangerous, just annoying. Although I don't necessarily agree with the path Tara took—continuing to live with Betsey for another year until their lease was up—she survived the experience seemingly unscathed. Once Tara discovered that Betsey was in fact a liar, she insists she was simply cautious about believing anything she said, which to me seems exhausting. (What'd Betsey say when she didn't want to wash the dishes? "No, I'm sorry, I can't. I'm fatally allergic to dish detergent"?) Perhaps Tara's a better, more tolerant person than I am, but I would've lived in fear of Betsey's lies eventually becoming more than just annoying.

It's hard to protect yourself from being fooled by a person like Betsey. You see, Sunshine showed warning signs from the very beginning; it was my fault for not paying attention to them. Betsey, on the other hand, revealed herself to Tara only after they'd been living together for quite some time. This doesn't mean that every girl will, at some point in her roommate career, end up feeling like she's living with a sociopath or pathological liar; it simply means that we often don't find

out what a person is really like until after we've already moved
in with them. As I said before, sociopaths make great first
impressions. Dr. Kulic says, "They're often excellent mim-
ics, and can read people quite well. Sociopaths are all about
getting their own needs met in any fashion possible." Their
lies are to crazy detectors as kryptonite is to Superman: They
render them useless. If a well-spoken, put-together girl we've
just met tells us she graduated from Harvard, and that she res-
cues abused animals on the weekend, why shouldn't we believe
her? Months later, when we're living with her, we find out that
she can't even point out Massachusetts on a map and that she
shudders at the sight of anything four-legged. As these truths
are revealed, the larger picture begins to come together—kind
of like stepping back from an impressionist painting: What was
once blurry becomes how-did-I-not-see-that-before clear—and
you realize that your roommate belongs in a padded room, not
the IKEA-inspired room right next to you. But, again, by that
point you're living with her, and although the last thing you want
to do is look for yet another place to live or another roommate,
it must be done. Tara was able to laugh at or ignore Betsey's lies
for the remaining year they lived together, but for most people,
there's an expiration date on that kind of tolerance, as there
should be. "If you start feeling like something's really wrong,"
says Dr. Kulic, "then just pull the lever that opens the trap door
in the floor and be done with it." The value of maintaining your
own sanity makes up for the cost of hiring movers.

The last story I've chosen to include here is one of *the*

craziest I've ever heard, and it happened to a person very close to me: my sister, Alissa. I had to include this story despite it being about a male roommate because (a) the content is not gender specific and (b) it's just so fucking bonkers. Plus, as my sister put it, this male roommate "had long hair and a pretty face, so he could have been mistaken for a girl from certain angles." To be more specific, he had long dreadlocks, which were part of his whole hippie persona, even though his looks weren't totally representative of his personality—"He was more of an art-student type than a functioning hippie," Alissa insisted. "He didn't smoke pot and he showered regularly." But he was still more free-spirited than most. For example, the first day my sister moved into the apartment, he was lying naked on the couch with only a sarong wrapped around his waist.

"Hey," he said, without even attempting to cover himself up. "I mean, his balls were touching the couch," my sister told me.

But despite his quirkiness, he was amiable and laid-back, and therefore pretty easy to live with. The following incident revealed the insanity that lurked beneath.

"It was about 10:00 a.m. on a weekday, and I had the day off from work," Alissa explained. Usually the apartment was quiet on weekday mornings after 8:00 a.m. because everyone had nine-to-five jobs. My sister would have been at work on this day as well, but she had switched days off with one of her coworkers; neither of her roommates was aware that she'd be home. She woke up to the sounds of beeping and sirens and voices on walkie-talkies. "I found Jason in the kitchen with a bunch of EMTs surrounding him and blood on his head." Police officers stood in the doorway, scribbling down notes on pads.

"What's going on?" Alissa asked, alarmed.

"Oh, I was mugged," Jason said. He looked surprised to see my sister but continued to sit calmly as an EMT inspected him.

"What?! When?"

"It happened last night, near the apartment. As I was getting out of my car, a guy pistol-whipped me and knocked me out. I woke up this morning, and my car was gone. I was disoriented, but I was able to walk home."

"Wait, you were knocked out last night and you just woke up now?" my sister asked, shocked. "Oh my God."

"So . . . about seven hours ago, right?" one of the cops interjected.

Right away, my sister found the story fishy. Not only did Jason appear inexplicably calm, he was also more concerned about getting a police report so he'd have something to show his boss—something that'd excuse his tardiness—than about getting his car back or the fact that he'd been assaulted.

By noon, Jason had been treated, and a police report was filed. His "stolen" car was found about two miles from the apartment, and the cops had a description of a suspect, albeit from their sole witness, the victim. Jason then got ready for work, equipped with the police report. But before he left, Alissa had a few questions for him. Well, just one question: "Did you really get mugged?"

"Ha. No," Jason said, without the slightest bit of embarrassment in his voice. "But I couldn't tell my boss the car accident story again."

"What? So you just made that whole thing up? How did you cut your head?"

"I hit myself over the head with a frying pan."

Jason, who had been freelancing as a production assistant on the set of a movie, decided he wanted to go into work late that day. *Not sick, just late.* Having taken excessive sick days in the past, he knew "a good story" was the only thing that would prevent him from getting fired, so he concocted this lie. What was almost as weird as the lie itself was how forthcoming he was about the details of his lie. "It was as if he was proud of the creativity he put into it," Alissa said.

In a *nut*shell—pun definitely intended—Jason woke up early that morning, drove his car to a desolate spot, and then took a cab back to the apartment. Once he got home, he went into the kitchen and hit himself over the head as hard as he could with a very large frying pan. Then he called the police. As far as Alissa could tell, neither the cops nor the EMTs seemed suspicious of Jason's story, not even the part about him getting knocked out for seven hours—a full night's sleep.

But wait, it gets worse: Jason's car was being held as evidence by the police, so he had to take a $150 cab ride to the movie set he was working on. Once he arrived, he was promptly fired. Out of money, he then turned around and hitchhiked all the way home.

My sister moved out shortly after the incident. As it turns out, the frying pan Jason used belonged to her. "When I was packing up, I realized it was no longer in the cupboard where I'd put it. I ended up finding it in the pantry, where Jason had hidden it in a black trash bag." They now live in separate states, but Alissa still talks to Jason once in a while. "Amazingly, he's not embarrassed about what he did. He thinks the story is funny," she said.

The moral of all these stories is that you can't fix mentally unstable roommates, nor can you make the situation work by, say, trying to avoid them. In fact, doing these things is only likely to exacerbate their crazy behavior. You must concentrate solely on saving yourself. Unless you're seriously, genuinely worried about your safety, you don't have to run out the door immediately in every case. It might be your first inclination (it was mine a few times), but it's not always realistic; what you should do is immediately start making plans to find another place to live. Dr. Lasky makes a good point: "You do not need to flee and put yourself in an uncomfortable situation somewhere else, but if you keep getting 'crazy' responses from your roommate, it is time to prioritize yourself and leave as soon as you can find an appropriate place to stay. Most 'crazy' people aren't dangerous—only a small percentage are—but start looking for new living quarters as soon as possible." In other words, most crazy roommates aren't going to kill you, and

most aren't going to be as evil as Patrick Bateman, but there
are plenty of things they can do to disrupt your life. Don't stick
around to see what those things are.

Things to Remember

* Ask the *right* questions before moving in with someone.
  (Do you party a lot? By yourself or with others? Do you
  believe in aliens? The E.T. kind or the little green men
  kind?) But don't depend solely on those questions to
  reveal if she's crazy or not; also spend time together
  before moving in together.

* Listen to your gut. The questions listed above can
  elicit very revealing answers, but spending time
  together will reveal more about who she truly is. Even
  if your prospective roommate seems to say the right
  things, pay attention to her tone, pauses, and any
  nervous laughter.

* Inquire about her roommate history: What has she
  learned from living with roommates? Where are
  some of her former roommates now, and what type
  of relationship does she have with them? What is
  she looking for in a roommate: a companion to share
  meals with or a person to share an apartment with?

* Don't attempt to cure a crazy roommate of her craziness.
  This will only make things worse. Just act as civilly as
  you can until you move out, which should be as soon as
  possible.

* Once it's established that your roommate is in fact crazy, keep your friends and boyfriends away. Exposing them to her, and her to them, will only make your exit that much more complicated and tricky. A clean getaway is what's key here.
* Some people reveal their craziness right off the bat—in which case, you can choose to not move in with them—and others reveal it only later, after you're living with them. Don't beat yourself up over getting fooled by a sociopath. It's what they do for a living (or just for kicks). Just move out as soon as possible.

Chapter Five
Too Much Information

DO be open with your roommate.
DON'T turn off your internal censor.

This chapter has purposefully been placed after "Idiosyncrasies or Idioscyncrazies?" because many of the people who share inappropriate information at inappropriate times tend to be a bit crazy. It's that whole not "adhering to societal norms" thing. But there are sane (okay, maybe just mostly sane) people who overshare as well, which at times can make for a very awkward living situation, especially when significant others are present for said oversharing.

Sure, everyone was raised differently and has learned to share personal information in her own way, but there is such a thing as sharing too much information (TMI), and I have lived with a few roommates who have completely lacked an internal censor. You see, there are plenty of girls out there who think that roommates should share the most intimate information with each other—details about sex, menstruation, bowel movements, STDs, you name it. But it takes a long time to work up to certain levels of intimacy, and while moving in with someone definitely means conceding to some level of immediate closeness, you shouldn't have to adapt to living with someone who's continually making you feel uncomfortable. "In any relationship," insists Dr. Lewis, "you don't spill your guts all at once. You start out cordially and pay attention to how your roommates react to the things you say. Paying attention to how people respond to you is very, very important."

> **Myth:** Roommates should be able to tell each other everything. On the 1980s show *Perfect Strangers*, Balki Bartokomous never censored himself, which often ended up embarrassing his roommate, Larry, but things always worked out in the end. Some people just don't know better, and you can't get mad at them for that.
> **Fact:** A roommate does not have to love you unconditionally. By not respecting a roommate's personal boundaries, you're only distancing yourself.

One of my roommates, Michelle, never paid attention to how my other roommate and I responded to her, because if she had, she would've noticed the shock and horror that came across our faces almost every time she opened her mouth. You see, she loved to talk about anything anal related, and she'd give monologues on everything from her bowel movements to her experience with hemorrhoids. I call them "monologues" because my other roommate and I didn't actually ever converse with her about these things. We just sat there, not even nodding, hoping she'd stop, which she never did. In fact, she didn't care who happened to be around to hear her, and I was embarrassed on more than one occasion because of it. One of the most mortifying moments happened when a guy I had recently started dating came over to watch a movie on our couch. Michelle walked in shortly after we pressed play.

*Michelle: Hey! Remember earlier when I was telling you about
    that hemorrhoid I have?*
Me: Um . . .
*Michelle: Yeah, so I was doing some research on the Internet
    and found out that people can get them from having anal
    sex. I mean, it's not from having a dirty butt or anything,
    thank God. My mom says my stepdad gets them all the
    time, and supposedly he has* **the cleanest** *butt hole ever.*

Then she poured herself a glass of water and walked out of the room.

My face felt so hot with embarrassment, it was probably the color of . . . well, a hemorrhoid. In contrast, the color had completely drained from my date's face. I had no idea how to explain what had just happened. This guy and I didn't know each other that well, but I was attracted to him, so I was obviously interested in making a good impression. How do you cuddle up to a guy after your roommate announces both her problem with hemorrhoids and her penchant for anal sex? Oh, and her dad's butt hole. It doesn't exactly set the mood. I tried to make light of the situation by rolling my eyes, but I knew what he was thinking: What type of crazy shit is this? If they talk about hemorrhoids so casually, does Amy have them also? Is she into anal sex too? And, maybe, Do these girls have so much anal sex that they both suffer from a chronic case of hemorrhoids?

Who knows what else was going through his head. It could've been even worse than what I thought. All I know is that Michelle's comments definitely affected him, because he didn't talk much for the rest of the night, besides to ask where the bathroom was, which he probably took refuge in to text his friends about the hemorrhoid-ridden girls he was hanging out with, or perhaps about the anal sex he thought he was going to have with me later that night.

I should've said something to Michelle right after this happened, something that let her know it wasn't okay with me that she talked so openly about "private" things when guests were over, but I was too embarrassed to bring it up again, even with her. I just wanted to forget about it.

Wrong solution. "Open, candid feedback needs to happen early on when you're living with a roommate who's sharing too much information," says Dr. Pass. "Confront her, but always use 'I' statements. Say, 'When you share that much information, it makes me feel uncomfortable.' Don't let the problem linger." Dr. Lasky concurs: "When you make a 'you' statement, you back the other person into a corner and increase the likelihood of a defensive response, a counterattack, or the person being too angry to speak at all. When you make an 'I' statement, you increase the chance of a dialogue, a conversation." Plus, it's tricky to tell someone who's obviously anal-obsessed that it's just plain weird, without hurting her feelings.

My roommate's anal fixation and her openness collided many times again, to the chagrin of both my other roommate and me. Another time, after she slept with a guy who happened to like having a finger inserted into his anus during sex, Michelle felt the need to spread the word. She went into full-blown proselytizer mode: "If you do this, your sex life will be infinitely better! Follow my lead, everyone!" And by everyone, I mean that she preached to people she barely knew, and she was aggressive about it. In fact, one time, while one of my friends was touching up her makeup in our bathroom before we went out, Michelle snuck in, closed the door behind her, and took a seat on the countertop.

Michelle: So, I have to tell you about this great discovery I've made.

Friend: Oh. What?

Michelle: You have to promise to try this with your boyfriend, and I'm telling you he will absolutely love it!

Friend: Yeah?

Michelle: Okay, so when you're having sex, you should slide a finger into his butt hole. He. Will. Go. Crazy.

Friend: [Uncomfortable laughter]

Michelle: All guys secretly love it. They just don't want to admit it.

My friend then excused herself from the bathroom and returned to the living room with an expression that said, "Oh my God, wait till I tell you what your crazy roommate just said to me."

Maybe Michelle was onto something—maybe if every girl stuck a finger up her boyfriend's butt hole during sex, it would greatly improve the sex lives of people all over the world. Who knows? I just didn't want to be near her, or associated with her, while she was on her mission to enlighten the masses. Unfortunately, she spent a solid month preaching about her discovery, following my other roommate and me around the apartment, moving her index finger up and down, like she was the possessed little boy in *The Shining*, except rather than creepily murmuring "Redrum, Redrum," she would repeat, "Have you tried it yet? Have you tried it yet?" (On a side note, I started dating another guy during this time, who before bed once overheard her preaching and said, "If I wake up in the middle of the night with Michelle's finger up my butt, I'm gonna be pissed.")

Eventually, she slowed down and stopped talking about it as much. We're not sure why, exactly. Maybe it was her inability to gain a bevy of loyal followers, or perhaps the guy she was hooking up with—the one who had once loved the kinky act so much—no longer cared for it. (I couldn't help but imagine him saying, "Okay, Michelle, enough with the damn finger!" She did mention how much he liked it once in front of a group of people, *with him there*, and I've never seen someone start sweating as fast and profusely as this guy did.) But whether he confronted her or asked her to stop using her finger during sex is just speculation. The point is, she stopped. And my roommate and I were relieved. But once again, we didn't handle the situation correctly. As Dr. Pass suggested, we should've taken the opportunity to talk to her about how uncomfortable the topics she brought up made us. She stopped talking about "the finger move" on her own, after all, so this would've been the perfect time to say something like, "Hey, I'm glad you're over that phase. It made us feel kinda weird." Dr. Kulic says, "It's easier to have an uncomfortable conversation with someone if you're genuine with them about your feelings and concerns without making them feel hyperdefensive." She probably would've been open to having this conversation, and less defensive, since she seemed to have realized—at least temporarily— that most people don't like getting unsolicited sex advice. But we didn't bring it up. Instead, we basked in her silence, and simply prayed that she had learned her lesson.

Our prayers, of course, went unanswered.

We enjoyed a few weeks of comfort, but then she struck again, and this time it was in a much more in-your-face way. After a visit to the emergency room because of a severe case of diarrhea, she returned home with no earth-shattering diagnosis, just doctor's orders to rest and drink lots of fluids. "That's good news for us," my other roommate and I secretly cheered. "She'll be confined to her room for a couple of days, so she'll have fewer opportunities to interact with our guests."

What we learned, though, was that people who like to share too much information can do so in a number of ways, ways that aren't always limited to the verbal variety. During a quiet little get-together (strategically planned while Michelle was out of commission), one of our guests was the victim of her openness, without Michelle even being present. When our guest emerged from the bathroom, he pulled me aside.

"Uh . . . have you seen what's next to the sink in your bathroom?" he asked.

"Oh, no," was all I could manage. I could tell by his tone that this was a you-have-to-see-it-to-believe-it situation.

"You should check it out. Like, right now."

When I saw it, I didn't want to believe it. I really, really didn't want to believe it. Sitting on the countertop of our communal bathroom was a medical-looking plastic bag with Michelle's full name on it. Inside the bag was a transparent container. And inside the container were Michelle's feces.

To my knowledge, doctors don't usually send patients home with their own stool samples. They keep them for tests and stuff. Then, I assume—I hope—they throw them away. Somehow, though, Michelle had been released from the hospital with her own stool sample—or she'd been asked to provide a new one later, and this was it. Either way, there it was in our communal bathroom. If my guest had seen an open box of Massengill on the countertop, that would've been embarrassing. Dirty underwear on the floor, gross. A Costco-size container of KY Jelly by the toilet paper roll, strange. But a bag of Michelle's shit on the countertop was just outrageously disgusting and bizarre. (Incidentally, months earlier, she had put her NuvaRing, the birth control she was on at the time, in our refrigerator. Apparently, The Ring is supposed to stay refrigerated before use, so my other roommate and I could excuse its presence. What we couldn't excuse was where she placed it: on top of a carton of our eggs.)

I couldn't help but kick myself after the stool sample incident. Why hadn't I said anything to Michelle earlier about her TMI issues? Why hadn't I done anything to prevent this from happening? By not telling her that her openness bothered us, she continued to think it was okay with us that she talked about and shared the things she did. Maybe confronting her would not have made much of a difference, or maybe she would've been furious, but maybe it could've spared one of my friends from seeing her crap on the countertop. We'll never know for sure, though, because we never tried. Instead, we kept our mouths shut and had to deal with a slew of these mortifying incidents until we moved out. (The night of the stool sample incident, my other roommate and I moved our little get-together to our neighborhood bar. By the time we returned home, the bag was no longer in the bathroom. Perhaps she finally realized what she had done and moved it after she had completely grossed out and embarrassed her roommates.)

Although Michelle was way too open about her love for anything butt related, at least she spared us any sound effects. Other girls aren't so lucky, particularly when it comes to the sounds of their roommates having sex. There's nothing wrong with having earth-shattering orgasms, but you should try to do it as quietly as possible when living with other people. Hearing your roommate's moans night after night is just . . . well, Too Much Information.

Beverly, a former colleague of mine, moved into an apartment with a friend, Katie, whom she had known for years, but it was only after they moved in together that Beverly *really* got to know Katie. Their rooms were separated by a very poorly cut door. "There was about an inch-and-a-half gap between the floor and the door, so you could basically hear everything going on in the next room," said Beverly. "Everything. Including the very loud orgasms she was faking on a near nightly basis." The guy Katie had been dating was nice and meant well, but was "basically a big loser." Katie seemed to be dating him out of sympathy, and she admitted to Beverly on more than one occasion that she never had orgasms with him. (He was also reportedly stingy in the oral sex department, which didn't help.) "It's bad enough to hear your roommate actually getting off, but when you're woken up by someone moaning and carrying on and you know it's all an act, it's even more annoying."

"Oh! Oh! Carl! Mmhmmm . . . mmhmm, that's it! That's it!" were the type of screams Beverly had to endure as she lay in bed every night. It was as if her roommate was reading (very badly) from a porno script.

"Finally, I confronted her," Beverly said, "and told her it was kind of annoying to hear her loudly faking it every night. The result turned out to be a win-win for everyone: She stopped faking it, he wondered why she wasn't so enthusiastic, she suggested a few things, he tried harder, and low and behold, we got a few genuine moans out of her." Beverly was still occasionally kept awake at night by Katie's amorous cries, but they weren't nearly as loud as before, and at least "they were the real deal." The way Beverly dealt with the situation was ideal: She wasn't submissive or aggressive; she was assertive (and threw in a little humor to lighten the situation). Dr. Kulic explains the difference in tacks: "Submissive people will often defer to others and assume that their own opinions are not important. They don't want to hurt anyone's feelings. They then become resentful because they never get their way. The aggressive person gets upset about things way too often and has to let everyone know how angry they are. They are willing to step on others to get their points made. They put others in a defensive posture. The assertive person, however, adopts just the right tone of caring and concern for themselves and others. It's a tough balance to be assertive and not aggressive, but the importance of being assertive is the ability to get your thoughts heard and needs met without subjugating anyone else."

Another one of Beverly's roommates wasn't even as modest as Katie was. "I walked in on her having oral sex in our living room once," Beverly told me. "She even knew I was coming home. But she just apologized and said that she thought they'd be done by the time I opened the front door." This same girl let her boyfriend eat a Gummi Bear off her exposed nipple while Beverly was in the same room—the kitchen, of all places— working on her laptop. "As soon as I realized what was happening, I shut my laptop and walked out," Beverly said. "Later, I approached both her and her boyfriend, who was over all the time, and said, 'Hey, I like you guys and all, but I really don't want to be so well-acquainted with your sex life. It's gross.' They laughed and said none of it was intentional, but confronting them seemed to work because I don't remember it happening after that."

It's simply not fair to expose your roommates to these types of situations. Seeing each other naked once in a while, or getting caught in awkward situations, is inevitable. But don't be sloppy or inconsiderate. The fact of the matter is, you don't live by yourself, so don't act like it.

Also, I suggest taking great care while indulging your sexual fantasies and fetishes while living with roommates, if for no other reason than it's apparently all too easy to lose yourself in them and forget that other people are around. Caroline, a friend of mine who lives in Boston, was truly frightened once because of a roommate's sex games. "I had just broken up with my boyfriend and moved in with this girl I didn't know," said Caroline. "The apartment was a one bedroom in the depths of Chinatown. The girl insisted she was going to convert the living room into another bedroom, where she would stay. She also said that she wasn't home a lot because she was always at her boyfriend's." It wasn't the ideal situation for Caroline—living in a one bedroom with a roommate—but it was a cheap and quick solution at the time.

After Caroline moved in, she noticed that her roommate hadn't even begun to convert the living room into another bedroom. In fact, Caroline wasn't even sure where her roommate was sleeping; there was no couch, only two large chairs. Also, it didn't appear as though Caroline's roommate even had a boyfriend. "One night I woke up to get a glass of water, and I noticed that she was sleeping upright in one of the chairs. It was really creepy. The next morning, I asked what was going on, and she said it was no problem, that she preferred to sleep that way."

"A secret lover is what she had," laughed Caroline, "and he pretended to break into our apartment via the living room as a form of foreplay."

The roommate's lover was a firefighter and their little sex game included him climbing the fire escape and then breaking into the apartment to save her from a fake fire. Although Caroline can laugh at it now, she was "scared as hell" the first time she witnessed this. "She never explained to me that this is what they did for fun, so I was freaked out, to say the least, when I saw someone climbing through our living room window," Caroline said. It was bad enough that she and her roommate were living in a one-bedroom apartment together, but it made things way more uncomfortable when Caroline learned of her roommate's kinky sex game. "I didn't want to see her sleeping upright in a chair every night, and I didn't want to see her lover breaking into the apartment as a way to turn her on. It was just too much information."

Listen, if there's any time to get crazy in bed, these are probably the best years to do it. Just don't force your roommate to see or hear you going at it. Unless she's a creepy voyeur, she doesn't want to know that much about you. The occasional moan or grunt is inevitable and excusable, but most room-mates don't want to be exposed to your weird, off-the-wall sex. She'll have a hard time making eye contact with you, and in the worst cases, she may have a hard time even conversing with you after learning about the crazy shit you're capable of in bed.

Nina, a writer, can attest to this. While living with a seem-ingly sweet and innocent girl (whose father was a priest and mother was a nun before they left their respective posts to marry each other—I don't think it's possible to be spawned from more innocence), she walked in on a bizarre, deviant scene. "One night," Nina began, "I came home late from work and imme-diately noticed that our kitchen table had been pushed away from the wall, and there was food everywhere. Then I heard Barry White—no joke—coming from our bathroom, where they were going at it in the shower." If the combination of scat-tered food and Barry White's bathroom crooning wasn't enough to freak Nina out, then what happened next was: "I thought I heard someone mooing, like a cow. Then the mooing turned to oinking, and before I knew it, there was a whole cacophony of barnyard animal noises coming from the bathroom. They [her roommate and her roommate's boyfriend] were totally getting it on while imitating the sounds of the animals from *Charlotte's Web*." Nina, of course, was horrified. I mean, her roommate knew she would be coming home at some point that night, so knowing that, why embark on such craziness? "I started slamming cabinet doors open and shut to let them know I was home, but they were unabashed. They were oinking and mooing and naying and making sheep noises." Nina couldn't bear to stay and listen, so she grabbed her coat and went to a friend's apartment for a couple of hours. "By the time I got home," Nina said, "the table was back in its proper place, the food was cleaned up, and the animals had gone to bed." Needless to say, after the incident, Nina had a very difficult time looking at her roommate without having flashbacks of what she'd seen and heard that night. (And forget about ever counting sheep again to help herself fall asleep.) "It was definitely the freakiest role playing I've ever encountered in my life." The whole situation made Nina so uncomfortable that she never brought it up to her roommate. Luckily, it seemed to have been a one-time thing, but even so, it changed how she viewed her roommate.

What's most unfortunate about roommates who share too much information is that they diminish the chances of having a normal and fun roommate relationship. Nina felt weird around her roommate after what she'd heard, and therefore

they never became close, and most of the conversations I had
with "I love anything butt related" Michelle made me uncomfortable, so I refrained from talking to her much. By the end
of our lease, I didn't even want to make eye contact with her,
which, I admit, may have been a bit extreme, but I was just
so afraid of what she was going to say and exhausted by trying
to figure out how to respond appropriately. She had said and
done so many weird, eyebrow-raising things by that point, I
was afraid of asking her anything beyond "How are you?" and
even that felt like a risky question at times. Says Dr. Lewis,
"Many times these types of people—the ones who share too
much—will perfunctorily ask how you're doing so that they
can launch into their own thing." I wanted to avoid that at all
costs.

Thankfully, my other roommate was very easy to talk to,
which is one of the biggest benefits of having a cool roommate:
They're nice to come home to. If a strange man approached
me on the subway (For instance, a guy in a suit on a crowded
subway car tried to strike up a conversation with me by using
the handle of his umbrella, which was in the shape of a duck's
head. "Hi," he said, as he stuck the duck in my face. "Hi," I
whispered back to the duck head, embarrassed and not knowing what else to do.), or I had seen something funny on my
way home from work (I once saw a yuppie couple in the West
Village who were screaming at each other about their wedding
plans as a small crowd formed around them.), I had someone
to share these stories with as soon as I walked through the

door. If either one of us had gone on a bad date, it was nice to know we could knock on each other's bedroom doors and vent about the scores of douche bag men populating the city. And our similar senses of humor provided a lot of comic relief in our otherwise stressful lives. I simply couldn't share these types of things with Michelle because she took everything too far. I didn't want to open the door to her unbridled candidness. Considering Michelle pretty much soured the relationship right from the start, there really wasn't even a comfortable place to go back to for us. My other roommate made things more bearable in the apartment because there was a normalcy to our conversations, which helped temper the weirdness we felt as a result of Michelle's monologues.

My friend Cara believes that having a roommate she could talk to led to one of the best friendships in her life. "I lived with two girls in LA, one of whom was much younger and did weird things like hum loudly to herself, talk on the phone for hours and hours on end, and never open the windows in her room, which resulted in an *interesting* smell. In the beginning, we all kept entirely to ourselves, but my other roommate turned out to be a lot like me and so we started meeting in our kitchen after work every day to chat. Then we'd eat microwave pizza late at night and drink beer, go to each other's rooms after dates to dish, and signal to each other while we called boys we liked to indicate how the conversation was going. Today, she is one of my best friends, and now that I live alone, I realize what a unique and fun time that was in my life." Because Cara and her roommate let their relationship happen naturally, without bombarding each other with personal information right off the bat, they felt comfortable enough to grow closer, to open up and share more intimate details over time.

Things to Remember

* Be aware of your audience. Just because you grew up in a house where people talked openly about, say, their bowel movements, doesn't mean your roommate is comfortable discussing such topics.

* Never discuss topics having to do with menstruation, yeast infections, or STDs around your roommate's guests, particularly if the guest happens to be your roommate's boyfriend.

* Solicit a close friend's advice on very personal matters before a roommate's, unless a mutual openness has been established between the two of you.

* If you live with a roommate who is "too open," politely mention to her that her openness makes you uncomfortable. While this conversation itself may be uncomfortable, it could save you from far more embarrassing situations in the future.

Chapter Six

Dust Bunnies Are Not Real Pets

DO share cleaning responsibilities.
DON'T wait for your (more Lysol-conscious)
roommate to pick up the slack.

To clean or not to clean, that is the question for many room-mates, especially when they're living with a roommate who cleans more often than they do. "Why clean if I don't have to?" they think. It's normal and should be expected that one room-mate is going to be messier than the other, but if cleaning chores become too imbalanced and one girl gets stuck doing all the work, frustration builds up, resentment grows, and, invariably, a fight breaks out. I used to have a roommate named Amanda who never cleaned the bathroom because she said she was never taught the proper way to scour that particular room. "My mother never made me do it," was her excuse. "I don't know how to." When my other roommate and I suggested that excuse was, well, bullshit, she replied, "Fine, well, then you guys just have to remind me each time it has to be cleaned so that I know when to do it."

Not knowing how to clean a bathroom is ridiculous enough. Not being able to recognize when something is dirty was just plain impossible for my other roommate and me to believe. Amanda would try to make up for her lack of cleaning by buying what I referred to as decorative accents: things like 2000 Flushes and Glade Plug-Ins. Now, if a bathroom isn't clean to begin with, blue toilet water isn't going to disguise that. In fact, it does the exact opposite. It reminds people to look around and assess how clean or dirty everything else is. And using a Plug-In in a dirty bathroom is akin to the guy who uses cologne to cover up the fact that he hasn't showered for a few days. On more than one occasion a guest asked us if we'd had an unsavory visitor recently. One more direct friend asked, "Okay, so is it a Mafioso or drug dealer who's been living in your bathroom?" What made the bathroom even more off-putting was the amount of rugs she bought for it. She threw little carpets on everything, even the lid to the toilet seat. (If Bed, Bath & Beyond had a senior citizen section, a place where they just sold home decorations to the AARP crowd, Amanda would've headed right for it every

> **Myth:** The neater roommate should do all the cleaning herself. That way, she can clean the apartment in the manner she deems best.
> **Fact:** Your roommate will appreciate your attempt at cleaning more than no attempt at all. Don't cheat on cleaning responsibilities.

time.) And the only thing worse than a dirty bathroom is a
carpeted dirty bathroom. The few times she did appear to be
putting some elbow grease into cleaning the bathroom, my
other roommate and I discovered it was all just for show.
We'd hear spraying and scrubbing, splashing, more spraying, and the occasional toilet flush. From the living room,
it sounded like honest-to-goodness cleaning was going on
in there, but when we checked the bathroom after she was
done, we still saw dust bunnies in the corners, dirt on the
floor, hair clogging the shower drain, and makeup remnants
on the countertop. And it's not like we were inspecting the
room with a magnifying glass. To the naked eye, the bathroom was just as dirty, if not more so, than before she had
"cleaned" it.

"What the hell was she doing in here?" I asked my other
roommate as we looked around.

"Pretending to clean?" she suggested. "It's like she hates
it so much she'd rather put more effort into pretending to do it
than actually doing it."

"Like little kids who run their toothbrushes under the fau-
cet so that their parents think they've brushed their teeth."

"Yeah, basically."

Her decorative accents extended to other areas of the
apartment. During what I refer to as "the Tulip Period," she
would come home from work with dozens of tulips and adorn
every room of the apartment with them. Buying tulips for the
apartment was a nice gesture on the surface, but not so nice

as, say, emptying our stinky, full trash bin. (She would, however, regularly hear my other roommate or me tying up the
overflowing bag and run from wherever she happened to be
in the apartment and grab a new bag out of the cabinet, as
if to say, "Oh, I was just about to do that!") She also bought
an inordinate number of kitchen accessories: spatulas,
tongs, oversize spoons, whisks, peelers, salad spinners,
fancy bottle openers, pot holders (in a colorful array of homey,
needlepoint prints), dishrags, cutting boards (both plastic and
wood), myriad cookie sheets and cupcake trays, and way too
many magnets for the refrigerator. These accessories, many of
which went unused, simply added clutter to an already small
kitchen. Rather than pick up after herself, she took trips to
Bed, Bath & Beyond, thinking this would excuse her from
all cleaning duties, as if my other roommate and I would say,
"Oh, let Amanda leave her dishes in the sink, and let's just
clean the dirty pots she left on the stove because look at this
great new spatula she bought for us!"

Not only were Amanda's "accessories" gratuitous, her
taste was downright strange. Although she had been out of
college for at least five years, she still had a strong collegial—
and sometimes just juvenile—decorating sense. In our mid-
twenties, many of us don't have the money to decorate our
apartments the way we'd really like to, but we at least *try* to
make our places look as nice and tastefully decorated as possible. Amanda, a proud postsorority girl, still embraced the
grunge and disarray of college living. Nostalgic for that way

of life, she forced it on my other roommate and me, hanging hip-hop posters (of Sisqó brandishing a G-string) outside our apartment door ("As a joke!"), and using a New Kids on the Block sheet ("It's funny!") to cover up the summer clothes and other miscellanea she stored underneath our staircase. In a college dorm or sorority house maybe these decorative touches would have been amusing, but in an urban apartment that supposedly housed "professional women," they were odd and embarrassing. A hot pink rendering of Joey McIntyre's face wasn't what I wanted to see as I walked by our staircase every day.

While my other roommate and I tried to make the best of our cheap IKEA furniture, Amanda suggested we do things like string Polaroid pictures together and hang them around the living room. And her decorating skills extended beyond second-grade arts and crafts to glorifying messes. One time, I spilled a glass of red wine on our white IKEA love seat, and Amanda actually got excited.

"Just leave it!" she exclaimed.

"What?!" I asked, as I pushed my way past her and scrambled to get a towel.

"Seriously. It's fine," she insisted. "In college we had a big booze stain on our couch, and everyone just laughed at it."

The red wine stain never did come out, which seemed to make Amanda exceedingly happy. I tried to cover the spot with a throw blanket, but whenever we had guests over, Amanda would yank the blanket away and yell, "Look what Amy did!"

The day she suggested we "just get a kitchen mat to cover up the dirt on our tile floor" was the same day my other roommate and I decided the only solution was to split the expense of a cleaning lady three ways. What I came to realize, as unbelievable as it is, was that Amanda not only truly didn't know how to clean but, more important, dirt just didn't seem to bother her. Even if we had wanted to teach her how to mop, she was incapable of recognizing the appropriate time to do it. In this case, a cleaning lady was the only solution. Sadly, we never did go about hiring one, which was a mistake because the cleaning duties remained seriously imbalanced, inciting frustration and a huge amount of passive-aggressiveness on my part.

In another situation, two neighbors of mine lived with a roommate who preferred redecorating to cleaning. They tried to tell her that a dirty coffee table still looks dirty whether it's beside the couch or in front of it, but she didn't seem to understand. When she was abruptly fired from her job, her redecorating escalated to an unbearable level for them. "Once, when my other roommate and I were at work, she actually spent a whole day taking the cabinet doors off the cabinets," my neighbor told me. "And we didn't have the type of kitchenware or cabinets that should've been on display." Their solution was to insist that she painstakingly reattach all the doors, which, they said, "seemed to teach her not to pull that crap again . . . at least while she was living with us." This same girl had the sudden urge to "make a garden" on our communal roof, which had a deck where we could have cookouts. Not many of the building's residents knew of her plans, so when extra-large black trash bags showed up next to the roof's grill, we were perplexed.

"What do you think is in 'em?" one neighbor asked, as he apprehensively untied one.

We all shook our heads and took a step back.

"I think . . . it's dirt?" he said after he peeked inside.

"Somebody actually carried huge bags of dirt all the way up here?" another neighbor wondered. "What the hell for?"

Later that day, we found out about the Gardener's plans from one of her roommates, who had managed to talk her out of dumping soil all over our roof. Unfortunately, the bags remained on the roof until somebody—not the Gardener—threw them away. A slob who experiences fleeting moments of ambition, like the Gardener, can be worse than a slob with no ambition because they create bigger messes. They're prone to starting major (usually ridiculous) projects and then abandoning them, leaving other people to clean up whatever it is they've left behind.

Messes, if you must make them, should be confined to your own bedroom. As long as you're not leaving food to rot in your room, be as messy as you want in there. One of my roommates lived amid piles of clothes, shoes, papers, empty water bottles, and stacks of magazines. Rather than pick a sweater up off of the floor, she'd usually just step over it or on it, unless she decided to wear it that day. At the beginning of each week, we'd joke about the type of storm that was going to hit her room in the following days, which depended on her schedule.

"This could be a level five hurricane week," she'd say if she knew work was going to be particularly busy.

We could joke about it because there was no bitterness between us; she was the only person who had to deal with her mess. In the common areas, she picked up after herself and made an effort to subdue her inner slob. I didn't care how messy her room was because I didn't have to see it.

A former colleague of mine, Jill, also lived with a slob, Carrie, who was far less considerate than my ex-roommate was. "She just wasn't a clean person," said Jill. "One day I came home and our whole apartment smelled like tuna. After a thorough search of the house I found an open can of tuna under a pile of dirty clothes in her room. Apparently she'd cracked it open for a snack and then forgotten about it. Truly disgusting!" Even though the can of tuna was left open in Carrie's room, the smell permeated the entire apartment. Yes, Carrie was being messy in her own space, but this type of messiness was affecting Jill, which wasn't fair. Also, the fact that Carrie had been sleeping in a room with an open, rotting can of tuna was unsanitary and weird. Putting your roommate in a position where she has to smell or clean up your gag-inducing messes is not cool. In fact, the only ones who will think it's cool are an apartment's most unwanted guests: rodents and cockroaches.

As I touched on with the Amanda situation, roommates also tend to get very passive-aggressive when it comes to cleaning responsibilities. I know from experience that doing things like washing only your own dish when there's a sink full of dirty dishes, or being especially loud while cleaning won't make your roommate want to get up off of the couch and help you. I had a roommate once who was always agitated while cleaning. She'd bang cabinet doors shut, sigh loudly, and slam pots and pans around. Making all that noise was her way of saying, "Look! I'm cleaning, and you're not!" But it never made me get up and help her. In fact, it had the opposite effect: Usually I'd just leave the room. Another roommate of mine frequently threatened, "I'm not gonna put a new trash bag in the bin ever again, because I'm the only one who ever does it." First of all, she wasn't the only one who ever emptied the trash, but it felt that way to her because she hated doing it so much. Second, even if she really was the only one who took the trash out, this wasn't an effective way to get her roommates to empty the trash more. The thing about slobs is that most of them are comfortable living amid overflowing trash bins, dirty dishes, and gross smells. You need to find something that they care about and subtly suggest the loss of that as a result of their messiness—their dignity, for example. Make your filthy roommate feel so embarrassed and guilty about being filthy that she's actually likely to do something about it. (Clean roommate to dirty roommate: I think I heard your boyfriend talking on the phone the other day about how our apartment always smells like a garbage dump.) It's still a passive-aggressive way to act, but you'll get better results than you will from, say, slamming cabinet doors shut, or boycotting taking the trash out. You can also use the "I saw a cockroach/mouse tactic!" which I've reverted to a number of times. Pretending to have seen mice or cockroaches in the vicinity of your roommate's mess (which, okay, you may not have to *pretend* to do if you live in a big city) will certainly encourage her to clean up more. Once, after Amanda left an especially big mess in the kitchen, with dirty dishes in the sink and leftover food on the stove, I told her that I had seen three cockroaches crawling around the sink—three baby cockroaches, which, I hinted, meant there was a mother with a lot more babies nearby. Of course, I hadn't really seen any cockroaches, but the look on her face—one of horror and absolute disgust—let me know that I'd made the right decision by lying to her. Within minutes, she was furiously scrubbing the pots and pans she had left in the sink, and in the weeks following, she was cleaner and more respectful about her messes than I had ever seen her be before.

Another (far more mature) solution is to create a cleaning schedule. It may sound like a corny tip from Alice on *The Brady Bunch*, but it works remarkably well. I, for example, despise cleaning out the refrigerator, but a roommate of mine found it "therapeutic." What she hated doing was washing the dishes, which I don't mind, so we each promised to take care of the cleaning duties we preferred, and things worked out swimmingly. Rather than trying to remember who washed the dishes last, or whose turn it was to take out the trash, or depending on my slightly sloppier roommate to *recognize* when something needed to be cleaned, we knew what our responsibilities were, and we were more likely stick with them because of that. This can be included in the contract Dr. Pass suggests roommates create before moving in together. Put it in writing, sign it, and post it somewhere everyone will see it on a regular basis. Like, right above the sinkful of dirty dishes.

Things to Remember

* Do your best to agree on what *clean* means—actually sit down and talk about it, and how often you feel certain areas should be routinely cleaned.
* Make a habit of cleaning the common area before you clean your own room.
* Clean up after yourself and your guests before going to sleep at night. Your roommate shouldn't have to wake up to your mess.
* If you're lucky enough to have a dishwasher, use it. Don't leave dishes in the sink "to soak" when what you're really doing is waiting for your roommate to load them into the dishwasher for you.
* If it's feasible and affordable for you and your roommate, share the cost of a cleaning lady. It'll cut down on a huge percentage of your arguments.

Chapter Seven
Boyfriends Without Benefits

DO allow your roommate's boyfriend to
stay over once in a while.
DON'T allow him to move in.

I've made the mistake of letting my boyfriends overstay my
roommates' welcomes many, many times. A lot of times
my roommates hadn't even welcomed (and on occasion were
openly hostile to) these guys in the first place, but I let them
stay anyway. Most of my ex-boyfriends are relatively polite,
congenial guys, but it was still annoying for my roommates
to have to deal with boyfriends who weren't even *their* boyfriends doing guy stuff in their apartment and generally taking up precious space. It's not that these guys would raid the
refrigerator, walk around naked, or hit on my roommates; it's
just that they were always over, irritating my roommates by
doing things like eating dinner in front of the TV, talking
loudly on their cell phones, or taking extra-long showers on

weekdays before work. One of my boyfriends used to lie down in the shower and "nap" for twenty minutes every morning, with the water on. Before I found him passed out, I'd always thought he was doing something much more salacious than sleeping. When I finally got up the nerve to check on him, it was a bit of a relief for me to find him like that. My roommate, on the other hand, didn't care if he was knitting or jerking off in there, as long as it didn't take him twenty minutes to do it. This same boyfriend would also help himself to any product that happened to be in the bathroom, including my roommate's $150 La Mer face cream, which—I came to find out—he had been slathering on his face postshave.

"Hey, can I find this cream at CVS?" he asked me one morning as he walked out of the bathroom. He had a glob of cream in the palm of his hand. "You're getting low, and it feels awesome on my skin after I shave." Then he smeared it on his face as if it were cheap sunscreen.

"What cream?" I asked nervously.

"You know, the stuff in that little jar? Why don't you buy a bigger container of it next time?

Once I realized what "little jar" he was talking about, I quickly explained to him that they didn't sell that type of cream at drugstores and, even if they did, he would never be willing to pay what they asked for it. I then forbid him from touching it again, but when my roommate confronted me about whether or not I'd been helping myself to it, I denied knowing anything. My boyfriend also used her Venus Vibrance razor to shave his

face, which she surely would've been upset about . . . if she
had ever found out. Luckily, I found it next to the sink covered
in his facial hair before she had a chance to discover why the
blade had become inexplicably dull as soon as my boyfriend
started using our shower.

By letting these boyfriends stay
over *all the time*, I was forcing my
roommates to live with an addi-
tional roommate—a roommate they
themselves hadn't chosen to live
with and who wasn't paying rent.
They were getting absolutely nothing out of the deal, except for the
occasional matchmaking services

> **Myth:** Your roommate
> won't mind if your
> boyfriend is always over,
> because it's good to
> have a man around the
> house—anyone can
> appreciate that.
> **Fact:** Having a man
> around the house is usually
> only appreciated by the
> girl dating said man.

my boyfriends offered, which consisted of something like this:
"Hey, have you met my buddy Jay?" And those services usually ended up benefiting only the Jays of my boyfriends' world,
who tended to be interested in one-night stands and one-night
stands only.

It's okay to let boyfriends sleep over occasionally (assuming
they're not sketchy), but to give them keys to the apartment, to
let them come and go as they please, to have them over more
than three nights a week, just isn't fair to your roommates. I
know many girls (some of whom have been *my* roommates)
who have agreed to let their roommates' boyfriends stay over
"for a week or so" until he finds another place to live, or a job,
or just a life in general. But that week or so invariably turns

into much longer, sometimes even several months, so if you're on the receiving end of your roommate's impoliteness, and if you find yourself living with a boyfriend without benefits, say something as soon as you feel that your generosity is being taken advantage of. Don't wait for your roommate to take control, because chances are she won't. Remember this: You're paying half of the rent and her boyfriend isn't, so she needs you more than she needs him. Ultimately, you have the upper hand. Don't be afraid to remind her of that; the consequences of being a pushover are grim.

If you don't stand up for yourself, you could end up in a situation like Lacy's. She was living in Miami with her best friend when the best friend started dating a total loser. "Like, I-have-a-warrant-out-for-my-arrest-in-another-state type of loser," according to Lacy. The loser boyfriend had gotten kicked out of his apartment for either not paying his portion of the rent or punching his roommate in the face. "It was never clear," Lacy said. Either way, the reason was dubious. He was supposed to stay with Lacy and her roommate for only a couple of days, but those couple of days turned into five weeks. "I was miserable," said Lacy. "He wouldn't speak to me, except to grunt hello. And he was emotionally abusive to my roommate. I couldn't stand him!" During the five weeks of the Loser's stay, Lacy's roommate found out that he had an ex-wife and two children. "She'd come to me crying, then she'd confront him about his lying, and then a few hours later she'd be like, 'Oh, we're fine!'" The whole situation was an emotional rollercoaster for Lacy, who hadn't wanted to go on the ride in the first place. "He used to yell and scream at her in front of me, and he refused to let her hang out with my boyfriend and me because he thought we were dorky." After five weeks the Loser left, and things were much more peaceful in the apartment, but the time Lacy had to spend dealing with him was emotionally draining for her. Imagine living with an abusive boyfriend who isn't even your boyfriend; it doesn't get much worse than that. I don't even think there are support groups for that kind of thing.

Here's another thing to consider: One of the reasons your roommate chose to live with you is that you're a girl. Many girls don't find living with a guy (other than a boyfriend) that appealing. Sure, some love it; others can tolerate it. But a lot of girls think guys in general are messier and grosser and, therefore, harder to live with. Your boyfriend is no different. "My roommate used to have her boyfriend over five nights a week," my friend Chloe told me. "He used to take really smelly poops in our bathroom, leave hair everywhere, and hog the remote control. He was a total couch commando. It was so annoying." Chloe was paying rent; her roommate's boyfriend wasn't, so why was he ever even allowed control of the couch? "I would get in so many arguments with him over the remote because he was constantly changing the channel to some football game."

If you have a serious boyfriend while living with roommates, you have to consider how much time he'll be spending in the apartment and how that is going to make your roommates feel. "You have to sit down with your roommates," says Dr. Lewis, "and ask them how they feel about your boyfriend being over a lot. Really pay attention to their responses. They may be afraid to be totally honest at first because they don't want you to think they're jealous of the fact that you have a boyfriend and they don't." When my boyfriends were constantly over, my roommates never explicitly complained about it, so I let myself believe that they were fine with the situation. In retrospect, I know they couldn't have been happy with the arrangement, and if I had paid more attention to the ways they behaved when my boyfriends were over (staying in their rooms a lot, not making conversation), I would've recognized that they weren't comfortable with the situation I was putting them in. To be honest, I was avoiding analyzing their reactions because that would've meant facing up to the reality that I was doing something wrong. And recognizing that you're doing something wrong is difficult when you don't want to change what it is you're doing.

Bella, an acquaintance from LA, had to deal with a roommate who, like me, refused to recognize her own bad behavior. "We were living in a three-bedroom apartment and we needed a third roommate because one of our roommates was moving to another city. We ended up finding this girl, Georgia, through a building management company," Bella said. "She said she had just broken up with her boyfriend and wanted a fresh start." Bella and her other roommate told Georgia that while they liked to have a good time, they didn't want anyone acting like they were still in college. They were in their mid-twenties

with professional jobs; they wanted a roommate who respected
and understood that they were past frat-party-type behavior.
Georgia seemed to accept that, so they offered her the room.
"When I called to ask her when exactly she wanted to move
in," Bella said, "she said it wouldn't be for another week or so
because she was getting her boobs done and wouldn't be able
to lift anything for a couple of days." Bella thought it was odd
that Georgia was so forthcoming about getting breast implants,
but she tried not to fixate on it. "It is LA, after all," she said.

When Georgia finally moved in, she had her boyfriend by
her side to help—the boyfriend she had supposedly broken up
with. After the first week, Bella and her other roommate also
found out that Georgia was far from living a professional, adult
life. "She was taking a random class here and there at a junior
college. That's it," said Bella. Georgia's boyfriend started staying over more and more, which didn't totally bother Bella and
her other roommate until about the third week. "At midnight on
a Tuesday, Georgia and her boyfriend were in her room, with
the music turned all the way up, having the loudest porn-star
sex," Bella said. "It's like they were doing it on purpose, putting
on a show. I started banging on the wall, to let them know they
were keeping me awake." But Georgia and her boyfriend kept at
it. The next morning, the neighbor from downstairs even mentioned to Bella that the commotion had woken her up. "I told
Georgia this couldn't happen again, that we had jobs we had to
wake up for and we couldn't be kept up like that, and that the
neighbors had complained," said Bella. Georgia apologized, but

just two weeks later, at 1:00 a.m. on a weeknight, she and her boyfriend were at it again: in her bedroom, throwing each other around like a couple of WWF wrestlers. The neighbor below started banging on the ceiling with a broomstick, and after about twenty minutes, Bella got up and knocked on Georgia's door. "She and her boyfriend just laughed at me."

It was suddenly like Bella and her other roommate were guests in Georgia and her boyfriend's apartment. The couple did what they wanted when they wanted, without any regard for Bella, her other roommate, or the neighbors below. When Georgia started complaining about not having money for rent, Bella and her other roommate decided it was time to kick her out. "When we told her she needed to move out, she didn't exactly take it well," Bella said. "That night, she came home drunk and started yelling at us about what horrible people we were. A couple of minutes later her boyfriend came storming up the stairs and let himself in with his own set of keys!" Apparently, Georgia had given her boyfriend a set of keys without consulting Bella or their other roommate. "He told us he had every right to a set of keys and could come and go as he pleased." When Georgia finally moved out a few days later, Bella immediately had the locks changed, but that wasn't the end of Georgia and her boyfriend. "While my roommate was at work, she got an angry call from Georgia's boyfriend, who had tried to get into our apartment to pick up her mail," Bella told me. "He was furious at us for having changed the locks! Who knows how often he had been in and out of our apartment when we weren't there." The smartest decision Bella and her roommate made was kicking

Georgia out and getting the locks changed, despite having to deal with the wrath of Georgia's boyfriend. If they had waited longer, who knows what would've happened. Georgia and her boyfriend could've converted the apartment into a porn studio.

My advice is this: Find out if a girl has a serious boyfriend before moving in with her. If she does, set ground rules before you're living under the same roof—that way she can't slowly sneak her boyfriend in until he's staying over five nights a week and then claim she didn't think you'd care because you never said anything. And never, ever assume that your roommates enjoy your boyfriend's company as much as you do. If you want your roommate to be *less* annoyed by the presence of your boyfriend, have him do little things that benefit her and the apartment. Maybe he pays for everyone's dinner (even just takeout) once a week, or takes out the trash, or fixes little things around the apartment—basically, clue him in to doing stuff that makes your roommate believe he's doing more than just taking up space.

Things to Remember

* Just because you love your boyfriend doesn't mean your roommates will.
* Don't ever give your boyfriend a set of keys to the apartment, unless you've first consulted your roommates.
* When your boyfriend is over, try not to act too couple-y around your roommates. It's their home, too, and they

probably don't enjoy walking in on you and your
boyfriend making out on the living room couch or
engaging in public displays of baby talk.

* Let your boyfriend get comfortable in your apartment,
  but not comfortable to the point where he's always
  opening the fridge or taking extra-long showers or
  "really smelly poops" in the communal bathroom.

Chapter Eight
Are You Gonna Eat That?

DO eat whatever you want.
DON'T make your roommate deal with your rotten leftovers.
DO share *some* food.
DON'T help yourself to food that's not meant to be shared.

One of my roommates used to save the strangest things in the refrigerator, such as a half-eaten can of corn with the fork still in it, two dried-up cherry tomatoes on a plate, rotting ginger root (which, to this day, I have no idea what she was planning to do with—it is, after all, a pretty obscure ingredient for someone who doesn't even know how to cook), an inordinate amount of Chinese takeout soy sauce packages (sometimes with only a drop left in them), and a mold-infested Costco-size jar of minced garlic. She rarely ate anything she saved in the fridge, but there her spoiled food would sit, greeting my other roommate and me every time we opened the refrigerator door. Her leftovers acted as a sort of appetite suppressant, so for that

I was grateful, but ultimately it was just plain inconsiderate.

This same roommate would also order massive amounts of produce from the delivery service Fresh Direct, which would arrive in stacks of cardboard boxes. By the time she was done unpacking them, our refrigerator would be overflowing with everything from fresh parsley to prewashed spinach. If she were a chef or an avid vegetable eater, this would've made sense, but she wasn't. I knew she did it because she liked the idea of cooking and eating healthily, but the follow-through simply was not there. To top things off, she felt guilty about not eating what she had bought, so it took a frustratingly long time for her to resign herself to the fact that her purchases had rotted, which meant that my other roommate and I had to sift through a sea of wilted green stuff to get to our milk or juice every morning.

Myth: If your roommate puts her leftovers in the refrigerator, it's because she wants you to have them. Otherwise, she would've just thrown them away.
Fact: If your roommate wants to share her food with you, she'll specifically offer it to you.

Just as frustrating are the roommates who buy obscure ingredients and *do know* what to do with them; the problem is, what they do with them can make you want to throw up. Roommates should be able to eat what they want, but you should know and acknowledge when your taste falls outside the norm. Foods such as fish, for example, should be prepared, stored, and cooked with more care than other foods. And if your roommate has an aversion to it, it's not fair to leave it sitting in the refrigerator for an extended period of time, or to store it in a container that is not tightly sealed. A friend of mine lived with a girl who would go to the fish market once a week, but she wouldn't always cook the fish on the day she bought it, so it would stink up not just the apartment but the building's hallways as well. "You could smell it as soon as you walked into the building," my friend said. "You can imagine, then, what it smelled like in our apartment and when we opened the refrigerator door." The fish was loosely wrapped in plastic wrap, so other foods in the refrigerator would absorb the smell of the fish, grossing my friend out to the point where she avoided opening the fridge at all costs.

The issue of sharing food is also a major one for most roommates. A communal refrigerator usually means you'll have to resign yourself to sharing things like milk and eggs. But there are boundaries: Some food just isn't meant to be shared, and other food is okay to share only if you and your roommate have the same definition of sharing. One of my roommates and I started off sharing things like peanut butter and ice cream. We'd take turns buying the items and replacing them once they were gone. This worked out in the beginning, but the way I ate these things eventually started to bother my roommate. "You do what I call 'eating in the round,'" she explained. "You eat the peanut butter and ice cream in such a way that round lumps are left perfectly centered in the container." And—okay, I admit it—ice cream is much less appealing when it's in the shape of a round lump, especially if someone other than you created that perfectly symmetrical lump. Once she brought it up to me, I was more conscious of not leaving lumps behind, but it turned out to be a hard habit to break (What can I say? I'm a perfectionist.), so we reverted to buying our own separate containers, which was an effective and necessary solution.

Another roommate of mine lived by the what's-yours-is-mine philosophy, but not by the what's-mine-is-yours one. She would help herself to others' Subway subs, entire pints of Ben & Jerry's ice cream (not even a lump would be left over), and countless prepackaged meals. If she happened to come home drunk, by morning our refrigerator looked like it had been attacked by a pack of rabid monkeys with an insatiable love for ketchup. What made her binges even more frustrating was that she was stingy with her own food. She would do things like store cases of Diet Coke in her room and bring loaves of bread to work with her.

When my other roommate confronted her via e-mail about a missing sandwich, it went something like this:

From: Hungry Roommate
To: Hogzilla
Subject: Just asking
Hey,
I bought a sub last night and put it in the fridge so that I could bring it to work for lunch today. Any idea what happened to one WHOLE half of it?

From: Hogzilla
To: Hungry Roommate
Subject: Re: Just asking
Hey! Maybe I had a bite. Sorry! I think I was drunk. I'll give you money for it!!!! ☺

Of course, she never replaced the food she helped herself to, nor did she mend her ways, but looking back, it was probably because my other roommate and I weren't firm enough about calling her out on her behavior. She kept doing it because she could. Even if Hogzilla had had the decency to pay my other roommate back for the sub, it still wouldn't have made up for her eating it. My other roommate had taken a trip to Subway, bought the sub, and planned on eating it for lunch the next day. Not only was it an unpleasant surprise to wake up to half of it missing, but it was also an inconvenience: Her new job was located in a place where there were very few restaurants and shops around, so she had to plan for lunch in advance. The six dollars she paid for it wasn't really the issue; it was more the trouble she had gone through to get it.

Many roommates make the mistake of thinking it's okay to eat their roommates' food if they pay them back for it, but money is only a small part of it. Think about this: If you return home after a long day, expecting to find, say, a Lean Cuisine meal in your freezer, but instead you find six dollars on the kitchen table from your roommate who already ate the frozen meal, how are you going to feel? Six dollars isn't going to cure your hunger pains, unless you go out and buy something else to eat, which is exactly what you were hoping to avoid by putting a Lean Cuisine meal in the freezer in the first place.

Ellie, a New Yorker in her twenties, had to deal with a similar problem when she lived with two girls who worked in the fashion industry. Both were fastidious about what they ate and maintained very strict diets. One of the roommates, Laura, used to eat exactly half a cup of Fiber One cereal every morning. "She would pick it out of the box with her fingers and measure it, like one extra fiber square would make her go up a jeans size," Ellie said. To burn off whatever paltry amount of calories they had consumed the night before, both fashionistas would wake up daily at 5:30 a.m. and work out at the gym for two hours. They were religious about their routines. Unless, that is, they happened to get fall-down drunk. "If they came home drunk, their diets went right out the window," Ellie said.[4] "I'd wake up in the morning and our kitchen would look like a scene out of *The Sixth Sense*—

---

[4] Drunk eating is an interesting phenomenon among girls because while we tend to be more disciplined, dietwise, than guys in our day-to-day lives, we can drunk eat a guy under the table any day of the week. It's a no-holds-barred type of eating that, if filmed, could be a *National Geographic*–worthy reality TV show. I've seen girls do things like squirt chocolate syrup into their mouths and then wash it down with straight-from-the-jug mouthfuls of milk, over and over again. I've heard what can accurately be described as growling from drunk girls when other people get too close to their food. I've also seen things like whole pizzas, pints of ice cream, and blocks of cheese disappear at an alarming rate. I've witnessed the ingestion of disgusting combinations of food (like cold SpaghettiOs smeared on saltines or mayonnaise and ketchup slathered on cold flour tortillas). I even saw one girl drop a piece of pizza on the sidewalk and then pick it up and eat it, without the tiniest bit of hesitation.

cupboard doors were swung open, leftover food covered the countertops, random concoctions of soy milk and chocolate protein powder sat in glasses, bags of chips were ripped open. They'd basically attack the kitchen." These drunken binges created a complete mess, and the worst part was that because they passed out immediately after the raid, Ellie had to wake up to these messes, and usually on a biweekly basis. "One time, I found Laura passed out on the couch with a half-eaten stromboli in her hand and pepperoni in her hair," laughed Ellie (who has since moved in with her boyfriend and can now appreciate the humor in her previous situation). Aside from the major mess the two roommates left in their wake, Ellie hated how indiscriminate they were during these binges. "They would eat anything and everything!" she said. "I would hide my peanut butter on the top shelf, pushed way to the back so that they couldn't reach it, but every morning after one of their big nights, my peanut butter would be open on the counter, with finger marks and unidentifiable crumbs in it. Yuck!" Ellie wouldn't have minded sharing her peanut butter with her roommates once in a while—like, when they were sober and remembered to use a utensil.

Equally annoying as the roommate who has no respect for boundaries is the roommate who creates too many. Like the roommate I mentioned earlier who hid cases of Diet Coke and lugged loaves of bread to work with her so that she could keep watch over them at all times, there are people who simply can't concede to sharing. I don't care if you grew up with five siblings and had to fight for and lay claim to everything you put in your mouth, it's an unattractive and immature quality, and something you need to get over if you're planning on living with other people as an adult.

Ashton, a twentysomething San Francisco native, lived with a girl who labeled all her food with a Sharpie marker. "When I first moved in and opened the fridge to find that she had written her initials on every single one of her eggs, I thought it was a joke," Ashton said. But the labeling didn't stop at initialing items. "When she ordered pizza," Ashton continued, "she would save what she didn't eat and then write the number of uneaten slices on the outside of the box. That way, she'd know if I had eaten one of them." Ashton didn't have the chance (or desire, really) to help herself to any of her roommate's food before the labeling started, but after she saw her initials on everything, she sure as hell wanted to start chowing down. While Ashton wouldn't normally have paid too much attention to things like a dozen eggs in her fridge, every time she saw her roommate's initials on them it pissed her off so much that she had the urge to make herself an extra-large omelet. Ultimately, the roommate's labeling achieved the opposite of what she wanted: It drew attention *to* her food rather than *away from it.* It also made her look like a complete jackass. At one point she even had a special frame built for her bed so that she could store food and other supplies underneath it. "She'd save things like restaurant napkins, ketchup and sugar packets, plastic utensils, and old wrapping paper," Ashton said. "She'd even take a roll of toilet paper in and out of the bathroom with her!"

It's understandable to be mildly protective of your food when you're only making enough money to feed yourself and if you're living with someone who's helping herself to your food way too often (and being stingy with her own), but it's totally off-putting to act like Ashton's roommate did. The fact that Ashton's roommate labeled her food was her way of saying *I don't trust you.* Ashton hadn't done anything to incite this sort of behavior in her roommate. And, moreover, it made Ashton *want* to eat her roommate's food, just to spite her.

But not all food-related roommate stories are as bad as the ones I've mentioned; some are actually pretty delicious. For example, a friend of mine lived with two fledgling chefs. They were both putting their time in at separate high-end restaurants, which means that although they worked unusual hours, they almost always brought home leftovers, the kind of food my friend never would've been able to afford on her own.

"I got to eat like a queen for free!" my friend said. "I'll probably never eat that well on a regular basis for the rest of my life. It was so much fun while it lasted."

Luckily, her roommates were happy to share with her. And there are plenty of girls out there who may not be chefs but who perhaps have Italian mothers who love to cook. Every time I visited my Italian mother, she'd send me back to my apartment with containers of chicken cacciatore and pasta fagiole. Not only was my roommate grateful when I shared, but she'd reciprocate by bringing back delicious plates of crispy dumplings and sesame noodles after visiting her Chinese aunt. Sharing food once in a while—especially when it's ethnic food home-cooked by a relative—always leads to healthier roommate relationships.

Things to Remember

* Unless you're a chef, keep experimentation in the kitchen to a minimum.
* Share refrigerator space as fairly as possible. Storing massive containers and cases of soda in a communal fridge should only be done on rare occasions, like when you and your roommate are sharing these oversize products.
* Save only the leftovers you're sure you are going to eat. If you do decide to save leftover meals, package them properly. Don't, for example, leave an uncovered bowl of tuna in the fridge.
* Don't be too protective of your food. That said, don't be afraid to say something to a roommate who moonlights as a hogzilla. Dr. Kulic warns, "Food equals money, which is often in short supply [when you're in your mid-twenties]. If someone is consistently 'borrowing' food from you, put it to a halt early and clearly, even at the risk of looking a little rigid."

Chapter Nine

Meeoooooow

DO take total responsibility for your pets.
DON'T expect your roommate to love or even like them, and certainly
DON'T expect her to want to clean up after them.

Owners of disruptive pets usually refuse to recognize how frustrating their furry friends can be to others. It's the same mechanism that prevents parents of petulant kids from seeing how annoying their children are to be around. Where others see nightmares, they see the most adorable creatures in the world. It's an important part of human nature, because if we didn't see beauty in our own kin and pets, who on earth would want to care for these little monsters?

When you're living with a roommate, you don't really have the right to bring a little monster into the apartment, unless you have your roommate's full consent. I happen to love animals, but do I believe certain pets should be off-limits while a person is living with a roommate? Yes. Should certain pets be forced to sleep in their owner's room rather than be allowed to roam around the apartment at night? Yes.

It's worth mentioning that the Black and White Report from Citi Habitats states that "only 7% of Manhattan renters have pets, compared with a national average of about 40% for dogs and 30% for cats." This isn't surprising, considering Manhattan also happens to be a huge roommate city. Of course, the percentage could be so low in New York City because many landlords don't allow pets, and the lack of parks and greenery doesn't make it conducive to owning them, but the fact that roommates and pets don't typically go well together certainly contributes to the low numbers.

I had a roommate once who owned a very cute-looking cat. The problem was, his cuteness belied his very, very evil spirit. He clearly suffered from some behavioral problems, but I wasn't knowledgeable enough about animal neuroses to diagnose him. All I knew was that as soon as the sun went down, this fluffy white cat turned into a furry monster. And I wasn't the only one who recognized this. Anybody who encountered him after twilight got to witness his demonic behavior. One friend caught the cat glaring at him while he was crouched in a predatory position. "Oh, yeah," he said, "you can definitely see the lion in him. If he were big enough, he'd totally eat us alive." The cat was most aggressive when I'd come home late and all the lights would be off. He'd hide in the darkness and wait for me to walk up the stairs to my room, at which point he'd jump out from behind the railing and ferociously swat at me. I'd scream and he'd run off, satisfied with his accomplishment. If cats could cackle, this is when he would've done it. His owner, my room- mate, thought this was cute. "He's just playing," she'd say. But being forced into the role of unsuspecting mouse every time I came home late at night wasn't my idea of fun. (It also wasn't my idea of fun to smell his dirty litter box every other day, a smell his owner was conveniently immune to. "I don't smell anything. I just cleaned it the other day," she'd say to my other roommate and me as we stood there pinching our noses.)

And while his furry white coat was one of the things that made him look so cute, it was also the one thing that prevented a few of my closest friends from ever stepping foot in my apart- ment, because they were so aller- gic to cat hair. According to the Humane Society, approximately 15 percent of the population is allergic to cats or dogs, which is something to consider before you bring a pet into a shared apart- ment. Even if your roommate

> **Myth:** The only person who wouldn't want to take care of your adorable pet is Cruella De Vill.
> **Fact:** Most people—even nice, animal-loving people— don't want to take care of their roommates' pets.

isn't allergic to your pet, chances are some of her friends will be, so if she doesn't already resent you for making her deal with living with your pet, she certainly may if her social life suffers because of it.

Despite the myriad problems my roommate's cat caused in the apartment, at least on the outside he was normal and therefore somewhat tolerable. I'll take a cute, evil cat over a kindhearted reptile any day. Sure, some off-limit pets can be lovable and fun . . . in their owners' minds. But to the people they don't belong to, they can be downright horrific. These pets include animals that aren't universally thought of as cute. (A good indicator is that they're usually lacking fur.) Snakes, for example, are at the top of the list.

In one particularly nightmarish story, a friend of mine was living in Baltimore, working as a bartender, and sharing an apartment with another girl. She and her roommate had very different schedules, so they went to bed and woke up at different times. One afternoon my friend decided to take a nap before going to work. When she woke up, there was a snake on her bedroom floor.

"Apparently my roommate had gone out and bought a snake while I was asleep," my friend said. "She brought it home, put it in its cage, which was right outside of my room, and then went out again. But while she was out, the snake escaped and slithered its way into my bedroom."

She then did what anyone would do if they woke up with a snake on their bedroom floor: screamed bloody murder. When she ran out of her room, she saw the new terrarium and concluded that the snake was her roommate's doing and that it hadn't found its way to her apartment by coincidence. After getting over the initial shock, my friend's fright turned to anger.

"It's just not one of those animals you can buy without consulting the person you live with," she said. "Suddenly we had this snake in our apartment, which made me really uneasy, especially since its diet consisted solely of live mice." The snake ultimately stayed, but the roommate relationship suffered as a result. My friend refused to care for the snake, or even look in its direction, and her roommate refused to return it to the pet store. "My lease was up later that summer, so I stuck it out for the next few months, but I made my roommate move the snake as far away from my room as possible. I always knew the snake was in the apartment, which sucked, but I rarely had to see it, which made it possible for me to stay there," my friend said.

My own sister, Alissa, violated the No Off-Limits Pets Rule by keeping two pet rats while sharing an apartment in San Francisco. (That bears repeating: *two pet rats*. And while rats don't lack fur, their tails do.) She let the rats, Felix and Little Vic, run around her room and asked her roommates to feed them—mind you, the rats followed a very complicated diet—when she went out of town. (The roommates agreed to feed them, but playing with them was out of the question.) The rats could do no wrong, and she occasionally let them sleep in bed with her—a situation Alissa thought was acceptable because they were "potty-trained." Her boyfriend walked around with tiny holes in most of his T-shirts because the rats nibbled through them—"a sign of their love for him," she said.

"They're lovable and social," she insisted.

"Yeah, but they have those tails," I reminded her. "And . . . they're rats."

Recently, Felix had a seizure and died a very traumatic death on the way to the veterinarian, while Alissa was driving. She pulled over to the side of the road and called me, sobbing.

"I don't know if he's dead or not!" she cried.

"Well, what does he look like?" I asked.

"Like one of those dead rats you'd see on the street."

"Uh, well, he's probably dead then. Ask Dad."

"Hold a mirror up to his mouth," was our father's suggestion. (Thank God our mother hadn't picked up when my sister called. A die-hard animal lover, she probably would've told her to attempt CPR.)

The results from the mirror test, of course, confirmed the worst: Felix was dead.

Because the rats were brothers, my sister thought it'd be healing to have a burial in her backyard. The fact that the service was held at midnight was accidental, but that didn't make it any less strange. Nobody attended except for my sister and Little Vic, who sat "somberly" on her shoulder as she dug a hole in the ground, placed his brother in a Nike shoebox (complete with mementos, like a wind chime "that soothed him while he was alive" and a Polaroid of him "on a happy day"), and then buried him. To this day she doesn't know if either of her roommates witnessed the makeshift funeral. Even if they had, I doubt they would've said anything to her, out of fear that she might ask them to attend a more elaborate memorial service.

A friend of mine, Victoria, owned an acceptable, roommate-friendly pet: a goldfish—three goldfish, to be exact. She bought a tank, cleaned it regularly, and took very good care of the fish that resided in it. Her roommate, Brenda, barely noticed the fish were there; Victoria had never even asked her to feed them. In fact, until the day Victoria spotted a new creature swimming in the tank, she didn't think Brenda had ever really paid attention to the tank or the fish. If the new creature had been another goldfish or even slightly resembled a fish, for that matter, Victoria would not have had a problem with it, but Brenda had added "this ugly, gross, wormlike creature with beady black eyes" to Victoria's tank without even consulting her. "It looked like it should've had legs," said Victoria, "but it missed the boat on acquiring them."

"Do you like the friend I bought for the goldfish?" Brenda asked Victoria. "I'm calling him Judge-Ito."

Not only were the three goldfish clearly disturbed by the presence of their new roommate (they now swam only together and along the periphery of the tank), but the creature would regularly jump out of the tank, despite the fact that he needed water to breathe. "He would 'pace' up and down the sides of the tank until the right moment presented itself and then catapult his body onto the floor," Victoria said. "The aquarium was in our kitchen, so I'd often find him in the corner, still alive, flapping around, all dried out with dust balls stuck to him."

The first time Judge-Ito threw himself out of the tank, Victoria grabbed his gooey body and threw him back in. "I really thought he had gotten the itch to escape out of his system," she said. "I mean, it had to have been traumatic for him—he had almost died. But before I knew it, he was trying to escape again." Victoria explained to Brenda what was happening (which she was somehow oblivious to), but she just thought it was cute. "Every time I came home, I checked the tank," said Victoria. "Even though I thought he was disgusting looking, I still felt bad for him." After firmly applying tape to all the tank's openings, Victoria returned home to a missing Judge-Ito again. "I looked everywhere, in the tank and on the floor, and when I bent down, I found him at the top of the tank, stuck to the tape. He had tried to escape. Again." As Victoria began to free him—for the second time—it dawned on her: *Maybe Judge-Ito wants to die.* "I suggested to Brenda that maybe the tank wasn't the best place for him—that perhaps he yearned to be slithering free with other wormlike creatures like himself. But she just laughed."

As time went on, and Judge-Ito continued to escape, Victoria was plagued with nightmares about him. "I had dreams that he was under my covers, moving his way up my bed, staring at me with his black, lifeless eyes," she said. "I hated that I had to save this thing over and over again—an ugly, slimy thing that I didn't even want in my apartment, so I stopped looking after him as much." Fate eventually stepped in, and one afternoon Judge-Ito was found in the corner of the kitchen, dried up and dead. "Neither Brenda nor I knew how long he had been there, but by that point, we both agreed that he was probably in a better, slimier place," said Victoria. Brenda, unfortunately, didn't learn her lesson with Judge-Ito and adopted another exotic pet, which she then ignored. "This one was a tropical frog," Victoria said "and it's a sadder story because when the frog started to get sick, Brenda didn't return him to the pet store or try to save him. She decided, instead, to *set him free* in the park, which sounds like a nice idea, except for the fact that it was February *and freezing*." Not only was Brenda a horrible pet owner, but she also picked the most obscure pets to bring into the apartment, which wasn't fair to Victoria, who ended up worrying about the bizarre creatures and trying to save their lives despite her feelings toward them.

People often buy pets because they think the pets will improve their lives, or perhaps solve a problem for them, like loneliness or . . . a mouse infestation. But they don't always think about the responsibilities that come along with the benefits of owning a pet. For example, a friend of mine, Jodi, is petrified of mice, so when she started spotting them around her New York City apartment, she called an exterminator. After a quick inspection, the exterminator informed her that the apartment was infested. According to Jodi, this is exactly how he put it: "Ma'am, aint nothin' you can do but get a cat. You got a real problem."

Jodi's roommate was out of town, so she took a trip to Petco alone, where she scanned the cages for the meanest, most evil-looking cat. "I wanted something that could kill," she insisted. Within minutes she came upon one that fit her criteria: He was black, paced aggressively, and had sinister eyes. "I brought him home and named him Julian, but looking back, I probably should have called him Satan." Within two days Julian had killed twelve mice, almost all of which had met their end in Jodi's roommate's room. "He didn't just kill them," she said. "He ate them—chewed them up and devoured them. I would find him postkill, licking his chops. It was sick."

Needless to say, Jodi's roommate wasn't too happy to find out that Jodi had adopted a wicked feline without consulting her, especially considering the kind of savagery that had been going on in her room while she was away. What's worse is that Julian had a difficult time digesting all the mice he was eating, so he'd regurgitate them. "One time I came home and he'd thrown up all over my roommate's rug, which was in the living room. The damage was so bad, I decided to just roll it up and throw it out. When my roommate came home, she freaked out. Apparently, it was a really expensive rug from her parents' antique shop. I had no idea; I thought it was from IKEA."

Julian also proved to be a problem when Jodi and her roommate had guests over. "I'd casually tell people that we'd gotten a cat, as a sort of warning, but I didn't want to scare them with the details. I hoped he just wouldn't come out of my room, and sometimes he didn't. But when he did, it was never good. He'd catch people by surprise, hiss at them, and sometimes even pounce on them." After just a few weeks of living with Julian, Jodi was scared to even walk to the bathroom in the morning. "I'd tiptoe to the shower, trying not to wake him, but being the predator that he was, he'd always hear me, then jump at me, with his ears back, and wrap his body around my leg, hissing at me the whole time."

Finally, Jodi had no choice but to return Julian to Petco. "My roommate and I were being tortured by him," she said. "The mice started to not look so bad in comparison, so we made a mutual decision to get rid of him. Pesky, disgusting mice were better than an evil cat." Chip, the Petco guy who had sold Jodi the cat, was surprised to see her back so soon.

"I think he has some sort of behavioral problems," she told him, as Julian squirmed and hissed in his carrier.

"Really? Like what?"

"I don't know. Rabies? Something bad," she said, as she handed him over.

Chip took Julian back, and Jodi left with a $200 store credit. To this day, she hasn't used the credit, but a few weeks after returning Julian, she received an e-mail from Chip. They'd found another home for Julian. "The new owner has recognized some behavioral problems in the cat as well," Chip wrote. "But she's going to try to work with him to overcome his issues."

Good luck, Jodi thought. *I hope she doesn't have mice. Or a roommate.*

Neither Jodi or her roommate ever got the chance to become

attached to Julian—there wasn't enough time, and neither of the ladies particularly liked animals possessed by demons. Aside from the missing rug, once Julian was gone, there wasn't much to remind them that he had ever been there. The guilt they felt for returning him to the pet store was minimal, at best.

In contrast, my friend Colleen felt immensely guilty about the situation her pseudo-pet was put in every day. The pet, a Weimaraner, didn't belong to Colleen or her roommate; he belonged to the roommate's boyfriend, who was never around. When Colleen's roommate first moved in, she asked if it'd be okay for her boyfriend's dog to be over once in a while. "I never had a pet growing up," Colleen told me, "so I thought it'd be cool to have a dog around occasionally, especially if I didn't have to take care of it." The dog, of course, ended up being at the apartment every single day Colleen and her room-mate lived together, and Colleen wasn't exempt from taking care of him. "The dog was sweet," Colleen said, "despite the fact that he was a manic depressive, drooled everywhere, and threw up at least twenty times in the exact same spot on my Turkish rug."

The problem, though, wasn't really the drool or the dog-gie vomit; it was the dog's morning routine Colleen loathed. "The typical day started like this: My roommate woke up and walked the dog. Then she left for work. I woke up after she left, took a shower, and got dressed. While I showered and dressed, the dog sat contentedly on the couch. But when I put my jacket on and grabbed my keys off the top of my dresser, the dog would rush to my bedroom door." (Colleen left her bedroom door shut during the day so that the dog wouldn't pee, poop, or puke in her room.) "By blocking my bedroom door, the dog thought I wouldn't be able to leave. I'd have to then put his leash on him and drag him across the hardwood floor." Once Colleen pulled the dog away from her bedroom, she'd have to run back before he did and slam her door shut. "This happened every single morning for an entire year," Colleen said. As a last attempt to keep Colleen in the apartment, the dog would then position his body in front of the apartment door. "I'd have to slide past this huge dog just to get out of the apartment every morning, and then I felt an enormous amount of guilt for leaving this sad-faced animal behind. He wasn't even my dog!" When Colleen happened to be running late for work, this routine was even more frustrating. The whole arrangement, ultimately, was unfair to both the dog and Colleen: The dog should've been with his owner, and Colleen should have been able to start her day guilt free. So just where was the owner? "That was the weird thing," Colleen said. "The dog was always at our apartment, but the boyfriend never was." It wasn't that Colleen didn't like animals, even, or this particular Weimaraner—she just wasn't ready to deal with the obligations of owning a pet, so the fact that she was forced to care for and feel guilty about one that wasn't even hers made her resent her roommate, who she never ended up confronting. "I mean, I *did* agree to let the pet stay over in the beginning," Colleen said. But like a Boyfriend Without Benefits, the pet became an unwanted third roommate for Colleen, taking up space and annoying her.

No matter which way you look at it, your pet becomes your roommate's pet too, so if you already own a pet, make sure whomever you live with accepts the idea of having a pet in the apartment, as well as the potential consequences and responsibilities that go along with it. If you don't already own a pet but you've been considering getting one while living with roommates, seriously think about the problems this may (and most likely will) cause in your apartment.

Things to Remember

* Wait to own an animal until you can afford to live by yourself.
* If you happen to already own a beloved pet, take sole responsibility for its care.
* Don't let your love for your pet cloud the reality of how annoying the animal may be to your roommate.
* It's completely unfair to expect your roommate to even tolerate being under the same roof with an off-limit pet. Especially if it's hairless.
* Don't attempt to harbor obscure, high-maintenance pets (like Judge-Ito) while living with a roommate because, whether you ignore it or care for it well, your roommate will inevitably have to deal with it too. And it probably creeps her out.

* As Dr. Kulic says, "Overall, pets are a bad idea in a roommate situation, unless there's a pre-existing condition. No one is going to love your pet as much as you do, which also means that no one is going to want to deal with all of the stuff that goes along with having a pet."

Chapter Ten
Borrowing Boys

DO be friendly to your roommate's dates.
DON'T flirt with or, under any circumstances, sleep with them.

For three months I lived with two roommates who weren't particularly fond of each other. On a superficial level they could interact amicably, but there was a fundamental dislike between the two of them that most people could detect after being around them for only a few minutes. Aside from what was just a basic clashing of personalities, they competed with and seemed to have a mutual suspicion of each other. Turns out that suspicion was warranted. Although they weren't absolutely certain of it, I think on some level they knew they were both stabbing each other in the back by sleeping with two of the same guys at the same time (who were friends and, not surprisingly, getting a big kick out of the whole situation. To guys, sleeping with roommates is almost as good as sleeping

with sisters). Essentially, my roommates had swapped partners without really knowing it: Each knew they were betraying
the other, but neither was aware that it was also being done
to them—blatant proof that karma is very real. It was never
clear whether my roommates wanted to *date* these guys or just
sleep with them, but both were rather careless about keeping
their betrayals a secret, talking a little too loudly on the phone
about their affairs, dropping obvious hints in conversations
with each other, and even sneaking the boys they were having affairs with into our apartment late at night. I was always
confounded by their lack of subtlety; it seemed to me that it'd
behoove them to be nothing but cautious about revealing their
duplicities. But they seemed to get off on the *idea* of getting
caught.

Of course, it didn't take long before the truth was revealed.
In fact, all it took was one of the guys walking out of my roommate's bedroom the morning after he had spent the night. My
other roommate was on her way to the bathroom when their
paths crossed. I had the pleasure of witnessing the "small
talk" that ensued.

Roommate: Oh, uh, hey.
Guy: Hiiiii.
Roommate: Are you? Wait. What are you doing?
Guy [Checking his watch]: Oh, actually, I'm just heading
    home. Gonna go meet some friends for brunch. [He glances
    out the window.] It looks pretty nice out today.

Roommate [Still staring at him]: Mmmm . . .
Guy: Okay, I'll see ya.
Roommate: Uh, yeah. Bye.

Obviously she was pissed off. But more so from embarrassment than the actual betrayal, I think. Yet what could she do? She had no right to say anything to our roommate because she had been doing the same thing to her. She did, however, make it a point to get back at our roommate by pursuing both of the guys like they were the last two men on earth. Once my roommates' betrayals were pretty much out in the open (the other roommate quickly found out that what she was doing was being done to her as well), the competition became even more intense, and the guys probably got more action during that time than they'll get for the rest of their lives.

It's safe to say that the only people who "won" in the end were the douche bag guys who were getting laid so easily. Honestly, I don't think either of my roommates even liked the guys that much. They seemed to be driven solely by the desire to get back at each other, which was ultimately a complete waste of time for both of them.

Borrowing boys or sleeping with someone you know your roommate has slept with in the past is a horrible idea, mainly because you run the risk of your roommate finding out and then using your toothbrush to clean the toilet. You never want to do anything to cause the person you're living with to be vengeful. In addition to causing a general sense of distrust and unease in your apartment, they have way too many opportunities to carry out their revenge successfully.

"It's reprehensible to be with someone you know your roommate is dating," says Dr. Lewis. "It's out of the question. Your values really have to be off to do something like this, and you should ask yourself what it says about you that you'd do it." You should also question why you'd be attracted to a guy who'd be okay with getting involved in a situation like this: "It says nothing good about the person initiating it or participating in it," insists Dr. Lewis. Dr. Kulic agrees: "Two things should almost always be kept out of close relationships: sleeping with a roommate's ex and sleeping with a roommate's current boyfriend. There are a few reasons for this, chief among them being that even if your roommate discarded her last boyfriend like a sack of garbage, you have no idea how she really feels about him, or what's going on between them still. Maybe he's just using you to get back at her. . . . This kind of stuff can get ugly quickly, and the best way to solve the problem is to avoid it entirely."

Not quite as serious as sleeping with your roommate's boyfriend (but slightly more creepy) is becoming openly obsessed

Myth: Any guy is fair game, even if he's dating your roommate. If he flirts with you, you have the right to flirt back. And if he's really hot, take it a step further. The girls on *Melrose Place* did it all the time.

Fact: The girls on *Melrose Place* were sluts, and their behavior was obviously meant to provoke melodrama. Seriously flirting or sleeping with a roommate's boyfriend is unacceptable.

with him. I lived with a girl once who became infatuated with a professional soccer player I dated briefly. The fact that she liked soccer to begin with allowed me to excuse some of her questionable acts, but when she started decorating our apartment with soccer ball–shaped pillows and all-star posters, I knew something was off.

"Do you know who that is?" she asked me when the soccer player walked out of our apartment the morning after he first spent the night.

"What do you mean? You know him?" I asked, a little concerned.

"Um, duh, he's only one of the most well-known soccer players in the U.S.!"

I've never really followed professional sports, especially not soccer, so while I was certainly impressed to learn about his athletic prowess, it didn't really change my view of him. My roommate, on the other hand, was completely and openly starstruck throughout my entire relationship with him.

The evidence of her obsession became apparent when soccer paraphernalia began cropping up around the apartment and when it escalated to her begging me to ask him if he'd play in one of her coed soccer league games.

"That'd be like my dad asking [quarterback] Tom Brady to play in one of his flag football games," a friend of mine said, laughing. "No, actually. It's worse. My dad's flag football league isn't coed."

I turned down her request on more than one occasion, but

that didn't thwart her plans or diminish her fanaticism. Whether it was buying soccer magnets for the fridge or calling her family members to tell them what he looked like "in person," she made it abundantly clear that she was completely enamored of him. And as I became more embarrassed, she became more brazen. One of the worst displays happened the morning after the soccer player and I shared a late night out. We were asleep in my room when we were awakened abruptly by the sound of her talking loudly on the phone. What we heard can only be described as some sort of homage to soccer.

"I love soccer. Soccer is my life. I would die without soccer. Soccer is the best sport man ever invented."

In some sick attempt to get the soccer player's attention, to prove to him that she was just as passionate about the sport as he, she decided to sing its praises as loudly as possible at 8:00 a.m. on a Sunday. Although I'm not entirely certain of it, I highly doubt anyone was on the other end of the phone. I mean, who could it have been? David Beckham? No normal person is willing to listen to that, especially on a Sunday morning.

The soccer player and I didn't say anything to each other about it, only because I know we both felt so embarrassed: I was embarrassed because of the person I lived with, and he was embarrassed for me.

As I mentioned, she became more brazen over time, eventually not even bothering to ask me to ask him to do favors for her. To my horror, she began to just approach him herself.

Not long after her Sunday morning tribute to soccer, she intercepted him on his way out of our apartment. It was early, and he had gotten up to go put money in the meter where his car was parked. She must've heard his footsteps, because she took off after him in her slippers.

"Hey! Good morning!" she chirped.

"Oh. Morning," he replied.

"Do you think I can get your autograph before you leave?"

"Um, sure. I'm actually gonna be right back, though."

"Okay! Great. See you soon."

I wanted to crawl under my bed and die. But I was too embarrassed to move. Instead, I pulled the covers over my head and cringed, waiting for it to get worse.

No way he's coming back, I said to myself

But within minutes, I heard the buzzer. He was back! *Wow, he must really like me to put up with this*, I thought. Then I remembered he'd left his wallet and hat behind. I buzzed him in but then sprinted back to my room; I didn't want him to know I had overheard my roommate's request. I was hoping he'd think she was the one who had buzzed him back in, and that I'd been sleeping the whole time. Again, it was just one of those situations that was too embarrassing to acknowledge. I didn't want him to know that I knew what had happened. Mostly, I didn't want him to think that I was okay with her being obsessed with him because then he might think that I had an unhealthy infatuation with him as well. My insecurity was obviously making things way more complicated than they had to be, but could you blame me?

"Hey. Did you have a parking ticket?" I asked in a fake sleepy voice as he opened the door to my room.

"Um, no. I didn't," he answered, in a tone that said parking tickets weren't his primary concern at the moment.

"Good."

"Hey, you know, your roommate's a little weird."

"I know," I answered quickly, hoping the conversation would stop there.

"I'm not at risk for getting killed with a high heel, am I?" he joked.[5]

"Oh, no. I think she just really likes soccer," I said a little too abruptly, and then pretended to fall back asleep.

The relationship fizzled not long after that conversation, and my roommate had a harder time than I did letting him go. "So, have you talked to him lately?" she would ask every other day or so.

"Nah . . . we've both been busy," I'd say, not wanting to divulge too much information.

"That's too bad. He was such a nice guy."

---

[5] In the 1992 movie *Single White Female*, starring Bridget Fonda as Allie and Jennifer Jason Leigh as Hedy, we see a roommate situation turn deadly. Hedy becomes obsessed with everything Allie-related. She starts to dress like her and to wear her hair like her, then attempts to seduce Allie's boyfriend, Sam. When Allie finally asks Hedy to move out, Hedy sneaks into Allie's bed one night and kills Sam by smashing a high-heeled shoe into his eye. My roommate was obsessed with the soccer player, not me, so looking back I guess *I'm the one* who should've been afraid of getting a stiletto heel slammed into my eye, not him.

"Yeah, well, there are lots of nice guys out there," I'd snap.

"Not like him."

The soccer decorations slowly started disappearing when she accepted he probably wasn't coming back, which was a relief, but any guy I introduced her to after the soccer player didn't measure up in her eyes. She had a hard time even saying "hello" or "nice to meet you" to the boyfriends that followed. Which, actually, was fine with me. I'd rather have a rude roommate than a creepy one, although I would've preferred just a polite one.

What can be even more annoying is when your roommate acts both rude *and* creepy toward the guy you're dating, which happened to my friend Rebecca. She and her roommate were both in their late twenties, had very time-consuming jobs, and were unhappily single. Generally, they didn't have the same taste in men. There were, however, exceptions.

Rebecca had a first date one night with a man named Ken she'd met a couple of weeks earlier. He was older, very tall, and recently divorced. She invited him over to the apartment for a drink before dinner. "When he walked in," Rebecca said, "my roommate, Claire, was in the kitchen. I quickly introduced them, and then Ken and I went into the living room. We were only sitting on the couch for a couple of minutes before Claire walked in."

"Wait, I know you!" Claire said to Ken excitedly as she came into the living room.

"Excuse me?" Ken asked.

"I know you! You're the guy I met while waiting in line to get into a stupid club a couple of months ago. You were smoking a cigarette outside and you hit on me, remember?"

"Mmmm . . . not really."

"Yeah, then I saw your wedding ring and I was like, 'You're totally fucking married.' And you were like, 'But you're so hot, why can't I just talk to you?' Remember?!"

"Oh. Yeah. Well, that was a while ago. I'm divorced now."

"Huh. That's what happens when you flirt with other women when you're married. I could've told you that," she said with a flirty giggle.

By this point Rebecca was having visions of the floor opening up and swallowing Claire. "I couldn't believe what she was doing," Rebecca said. "My face must've been purple with anger, and Ken was clearly embarrassed." Was Claire flirting or being a bitch? Rebecca couldn't tell. It seemed to be a weird combination of both. "Heavy flirting puts your roommate and her boyfriend in an uncomfortable situation. It also raises questions of where your loyalty lies," says Dr. Lasky. Claire continued to reminisce about their night in the club line, until Rebecca finally interrupted her. "Claire, can I talk to you for a minute?"

"Okay," she said, but it was obvious she didn't want to leave the room.

"What the hell are you doing?" Rebecca asked, once they were out of Ken's earshot.

"Rebecca, he's too tall for you" was all Claire said.

"What?!"

Claire was about five foot nine, which is definitely taller for a girl, but not so tall that she had a hard time getting dates because of it. She regularly complained to five foot three Rebecca that the selection of guys was much smaller for tall girls like her, and it was "really a problem for her and her long legs."

"Rebecca, you're short. You have no right dating someone as tall as him. There aren't a lot of guys out there for girls my height. It is not fair for you to dip into our dating pool."

Rebecca couldn't believe what she was hearing, so she just walked away and left the apartment with Tall Ken. Neither of them said good-bye to Tall Claire.

Ultimately, things didn't work out between Rebecca and Ken. But that's not what's important here; what matters is that Claire, for some reason, thought it was her job to tell Rebecca whom she could and could not date. And Claire's attempt to sabotage Rebecca's relationship with Ken from the very beginning was just a low blow. Now, someone in Claire's position, with better intentions, may have been inclined to pull Rebecca aside and tell her that he'd hit on her pretty aggressively while he had a wedding ring on his finger—a good indicator that he may not be a stand-up guy, but the way Claire went about calling Ken out put everyone on the defensive, including Rebecca. It made Rebecca feel like Claire was competing with her, not helping her.

Competition among female roommates is inevitable, but there are ways to prevent it from getting out of hand, one of which is to leave each other's boyfriends alone. So many disasters can result from flirting or going after guys your roommate is involved with, it's just not worth the trouble. Not only are there plenty of other guys to choose from besides your roommate's boyfriend, there are also plenty of other girls to compete with besides your roommate. Why bring ugly, uncomfortable competition like that into the place you live? No matter how hot or perfect you think your roommate's guy is, no matter how many signals you think he's sending you, don't pursue him in any way.

Sharing boy *stories*, however, is totally encouraged. Roommates are often the best people to share these experiences with because they can attach a face to the story. Unlike some of your girlfriends, your roommate is more privy to your boy's behaviors: She witnesses things like how he acts when he leaves in the morning, the way he dresses, and whether or not he's considerate enough to put the toilet seat down after going to the bathroom. Of course it's always fun to talk about The Morning After with girlfriends, but it can be even more fun to talk about it while you're still in your pajamas, and with the first person you see: your roommate. If you're comfortable enough to share the salacious details with each other, Sunday morning coffee on the couch can be highly entertaining. Claire's need to compete with Georgia, for example, was unfortunate because roommates can be great people to go to for advice on the guys you date. If they have you in their best interest, and they're not set on stealing your guy, their advice can be more insightful and helpful than even a best friend's can be.

Things to Remember

* There are plenty of guys to go around. Find your own boyfriend to play with.
* Developing a crush on your roommate's boyfriend sometimes just happens, especially if that boyfriend happens to be a really good-looking professional athlete. But keep your crush in check. Confess your feelings to your journal, or laugh about it to a close friend. Never, ever act on it in any way. As Dr. Lewis says, "It's simply out of the question. Period."
* Even if your roommate claims to be "over" a guy, stay away from him, at least until you aren't living under the same roof as his ex.
* As clever and sneaky as you think you are, even a skilled magician would have a hard time surreptitiously stealing her roommate's boyfriend and getting away with it. The chances of you getting caught "borrowing" your roommate's boyfriend are way too high.
* Share boyfriend stories, not boyfriends, with your roommate. Because she's experienced more of your boyfriend's behaviors than most of your girlfriends have, she can often offer better insight and advice.

Chapter Eleven
Hangover Hell

DO exercise the right to be hungover.
DON'T force your roommate to suffer
through a vicarious hangover.

One of my roommates used to deal with her hangovers so badly that she'd make me feel like I was hungover too, even if I hadn't enjoyed the benefit of getting drunk the night before.

"I don't know why I feel so bad," she'd whine, languidly stretched out on the couch, remote in one hand, French fries in the other.

"Well, what'd you do last night?" I'd ask, knowing she probably drank enough to intoxicate an entire sorority house at one of the country's biggest party schools.

"Oh my God, it was so fun. We went to this new bar, and these guys just kept buying us tequila shots!"

"Really? And you feel like shit? Strange. Oh, and you

don't remember the last half of your night? Even stranger."

You're not in college anymore, which isn't to suggest you can't still drink like you are once in a while. But you're old enough to know that you're going to pay the price the next day. Don't make your roommates suffer with you. And never, ever ask: "What's wrong with me? Why do I feel this way?"

Myth: If your roommate has ever had a hangover, she will have complete compassion for you when you're going through one, even if you complain profusely.
Fact: Complaining about being hungover will seriously deplete whatever compassion your roommate feels toward you.

Girls do all sorts of things when they're drunk that they totally regret the next day. Although it might not feel like it when you're hungover, you will survive both the headache and the humiliation of whatever you did the night before. Take comfort in the fact that following a night of heavy drinking, most girls in their twenties would be able to put a check next to at least some of the following alcohol-induced activities:

* Made out with a random guy
* Made out with a random guy in public
* Woke up next to a random guy
* Ate way too much way too late
* Put foot in mouth, not once, not twice, but all night long
* Threw up on a sidewalk
* Threw up in a cab

* Got thrown out of a cab
* Drunk-dialed an ex
* Drunk-dialed multiple exes
* Drunk-dialed Mom and/or Dad
* Screamed, "I don't wait in line to get into clubs!" while waiting in line to get into clubs
* Danced on a table
* Danced on what appeared at the time to be a table
* Tripped and fell
* Tripped and fell in front of a *huge* group of people
* Got in a fight
* Lost a cell phone
* Lost a wallet
* Lost a shoe
* Said "I love you" way too frequently and without discretion
* Said "I hate you" way too frequently and without discretion
* Threw up in another cab

Waking up to the realization that you've committed most, if not all, of the above acts can be very painful; I'm not arguing with that. But what you have to remember is that you're too old to cry about it. Sure, whine a little, seek comfort in your friends' and roommates' advice and their I've-been-there-before stories, but then get over it. Don't drag everyone in the apartment down with you. You're too old to think that a hangover is the end of your life. You've suffered through too many of them in the past to not know that you'll get over it.

One roommate of mine had a particularly difficult time dealing with her hangovers, mainly because she started experimenting with drugs when she was way past the experimental age. It made my other roommate and me nervous because she didn't know her limits. At her age, she didn't have parents waiting up for her who would ground her if she came home late with dilated pupils, or teachers who would order drug tests if she acted funny in class. She was an adult, but she was trying drugs with the naïveté of a teenager. Her hangovers, not surprisingly, were melodramatic and over-the-top. On Sunday mornings she'd take trips to the emergency room "for headaches and cold sweats" or sulk around the apartment and wonder why she was "soooo depressed." Rather than attribute her morning-after symptoms to the partying she had done the night before, she'd blame them on "some crazy flu" or "severe food poisoning." It was annoying for my other roommate and me because she never learned her lesson—which was that if you drink and do drugs, you're going to feel like shit the next day. You haven't been struck with a mutant strain of the Ebola virus or a sudden case of Lyme disease; you're simply hungover, even if your symptoms resemble those associated with the plague. If you can't keep things in perspective, then don't allow yourself to get that intoxicated. It's as simple as that.

In addition to her annoying, hangover-induced hypochondria, her whining made the hangovers my other roommate and

I suffered from exponentially worse; the energy we needed to get over our own headaches and nausea was wasted trying to convince her that she wasn't dying. Here's an example of just how painful she was to deal with. One morning when we were hung over, a few neighbors came over to rehash the events from a party we'd had on our roof the night before. We all sat in the living room with headaches and sour stomachs and pieced together our memories of the night before. Whiny Roommate emerged from her room looking like hell. "Oh my God," she said, with her hand on her head.

"I feel ya," a neighbor chimed in. "We're all in the same boat."

"I think I'm really sick," she said. "Is the flu going around?"

"Yeah, the Irish flu," someone called out, laughing.

"No. I really *do not* feel well," she insisted, and went into the bathroom and slammed the door.

"Is she joking?" another neighbor asked. "Last time I saw her it was 3:00 a.m. and she was pounding tequila shots."

"She does this all the time," I said. "It's like she refuses to believe that she brought this pain on herself so she blames it on something else, like the flu."

The rest of us ordered pizza and continued to lounge around and watch TV. Whiny Roommate returned a while later, fully dressed and on the verge of tears. "You guys, I just feel really bad."

Nobody said anything.

She walked across the room and sat on the windowsill. (The window and screen were open.) "I'm just really, really depressed," she continued, as she stared down at the street below. We all looked at her, but still, nobody said anything. The awkwardness was palpable. My other roommate and I had experienced this melodrama before, but our neighbors were freaked out. Who walks into a quiet room filled with people watching TV and announces that they're depressed? Oh, and then sits next to an open window while gazing down at the street below? Nobody said anything for a good five minutes, which seemed to aggravate her even more.

"Is she going to jump?" one of the neighbors mouthed to me from across the room.

I rolled my eyes and shook my head.

Finally, Whiny Roommate got up, sighed loudly, mumbled something about going to church, and left.

"Is she okay?" another neighbor asked once she was gone.

"Yes," my other roommate and I said together, annoyed, knowing this wasn't a cry for help, but her morning-after M.O.

Not only did Whiny Roommate make things worse for my other roommate and me, she also made things worse for herself because she couldn't benefit from hangover advice, and she refused to accept and deal with the hangover. ("It's better to give in to the hangover than to resist it," one of my friends always says.)

On days when she happened to be hungover and my other

roommate and I weren't, things could be just as bad. In addition to whining and complaining, she also almost never picked up after herself. When we wanted to open the blinds to let the sun in, she wanted to keep them drawn. When we wanted to turn off the TV and play music, she'd want to stay on the couch all day watching movies. It was the land of the dead versus the land of the living, and the dead almost always won out. So just try not to make your roommate suffer on a day when she wants to celebrate her health, which can be a rare occurrence for a single girl in her twenties.

That said, if you and your roommate both happen to be hungover, there's nothing better than commiserating with each other. If you lived by yourself, you'd have to suffer through what my friends and I refer to as the Morning-After Meltdown all alone. One of my roommates and I were almost always hungover on the same days. ("The Serendipitous Hangover," we called it.) It significantly alleviated the pain of our hangovers because we could take turns getting off the couch to pay the food delivery guy, and we could watch cheesy eighties movies together all day, something that just doesn't yield the same satisfaction when done alone. The Serendipitous Hangover also defused some of the guilt of being hungover. We could laugh with each other about the stupid things we had done the night before rather than sit alone and brood over them. If you drunk-dialed your ex-boyfriend fifteen times in a row, you won't feel as bad about it if you know your roommate drunk-dialed hers thirty times in just ten minutes.

Things to Remember

* If you're so hungover that the only sounds you can make are guttural moans, just stay in your room.

* If you do venture out to the common area, keep your complaining to a minimum. Sure, feel free to express the magnitude of your hangover, once. After that, let your sallow skin and vodka-infused odor convey the message. Physical manifestations of a hangover are much more powerful than words.

* If you're the victim of your roommate's complaining, don't feel bad about using tactics—like acting extraordinarily happy and perky—to force her back into her room. Perhaps remind her that she looks (and smells) like hell too.

* Don't act like you're sick with the flu when both you and your roommate know you're merely suffering from a hangover. It's immature, and the next time you actually are suffering from the flu your roommate will be less likely to go to the store to pick up ginger ale and saltines for you since you've cried wolf so many times.

Chapter Twelve

Sex, Drugs, & Roommates Who Party Like Rock Stars

DO have fun in your own apartment.
DON'T expect that your roommate's
idea of fun is the same as yours.

When you first meet a person who likes to party and is always up for a good time, it's hard not to like them. Their energy is contagious, they surround themselves with people who share their joie de vivre, they make you feel alive, and they're highly, sometimes addictively, entertaining. The problem with many of these people is that they have a hard time turning the party switch off, so living with them can be maddening after a while. As roommates, over time, they can make you feel the opposite of alive, like if you spend one more night around them, the Grim Reaper is going to show up at your front door. "Death by association," he'll say, as he rounds up everyone in the apartment. "Let's go."

Here's the thing about partying while living with roommates:

There are going to be nights when you're in bed early and one of your roommates and her friends are up too late. They'll be too loud, the door will keep slamming, cell phones will keep ringing, and the volume on the TV and/or stereo will continue to be turned up. Yet if you want to earn some of your own free nights of doing the same thing, you have to keep your mouth shut. That said, there are lines roommates simply should not cross, and perpetual partiers, the people you liked so much when you first met them, have a hard time discerning where that line is.

I once had a roommate who put sex at the very top of her list of Fun Recreational Activities. In other words, she had a lot of it, with a lot of different guys. The noises that came out of her room during her sexual escapades often sounded more like a wrestling match than two people being intimate. The first few times it happened, my other roommate and I didn't know if we should check on her. We'd hear glass breaking, pictures falling off their hooks, and her headboard banging against the wall. Then her bedroom door would swing open and a fully naked guy would walk out, sometimes even still with an erection, nod hello to my other roommate and me, and stroll into the bathroom. (This happened once when my other roommate and I came home late from being out. Drunk and hungry, we decided to microwave some hot dogs. As soon as we started to eat them, a guy emerged from our roommate's room, naked and with an erect penis. Like a couple of junior high girls, we got a huge kick out of seeing a real-life penis juxtaposed with the hot dogs we had just bitten into. We laughed so hard my roommate started to choke and then almost threw up.) As time went on, we came to expect this type of thing—that is, postcoital naked guys strolling into our bathroom late at night—but we never got used to it. Sex was this girl's idea of fun. Some people blow off steam by drinking, or let loose by dancing on tables. This girl went wild in the bedroom.

"How was your night?" we would ask her the next morning, looking for some acknowledgement from her that things had gotten a little out of control.

"Fine," she'd say curtly, and then walk away. Perhaps she was embarrassed, but she never apologized for having sex that hit 8.0 on the Richter scale. Luckily for my other roommate and me, the guys she brought home were all smokin' hot, so at least they were nice to look at, clothed or not.

Again, I was lucky because my roommate liked to get frisky with good-looking, upstanding members of society. Other girls aren't so lucky and get stuck living with girls who are not at all discriminating about the guys they bring home.

A friend of mine was sharing an apartment with a girl in New York City who brought home all sorts of guys from all walks of life. One night, for example, she woke up in the middle of the night to a German shepherd breathing in her ear. Her screams woke up her roommate, who then stumbled into her room.

"Oh, sorry," said a heavily accented male voice behind her roommate. "He's mine. I wasn't keeping an eye on him."

"So, in the middle of the night," my friend said, "I had

both a strange dog and a strange man in my bedroom. Oh, and a drunk roommate."

The man turned out to be a cab driver her roommate had met on her way home from a bar. They'd started flirting in the cab, and she invited him back to the apartment. He agreed, on the condition that he could pick up his dog at home and bring him along.

> **Myth:** Like *The Real World*, your apartment should be the central party place for you and your roommates. You're young, there's no parental guidance, so go for it.
> **Fact:** Using your living space for parties is what dorm rooms (and *The Real World* house) are for. In a shared apartment, occasional get-togethers are fine. Weekly swinging-from-the-rafters parties: not fine at all.

"It wasn't exactly smart of her to bring a guy back to the apartment who she had just met, especially considering how drunk she was," my friend said. "Plus, what kind of weirdo insists on bringing his dog—his very *big* dog—with him?"

Even if you're willing to put yourself in a dangerous, dubious, or awkward situation, that doesn't mean your roommate is. So try to consider her feelings before bringing home a random man (and his pet). The bottom line is, you need to be up front with your roommate about who is allowed to come and go and when, since your personal safety, or at the very least your relationship with your landlord, is at stake when she lets strangers (and strange animals) into your apartment. People can get hurt, things can get stolen, and cabinets can get chewed up. And this advice applies when you're not at home too.

One ex-roommate of mine lent our apartment keys to an ex-boyfriend for the day once. Unbeknownst to me, she had agreed to let him and his punk rock band shoot a video on our roof. So, in the middle of the day, while I was working from home, in walked three heavily tattooed musicians accompanied by two girls in what can only be described as stripper garb.

"Oh. Hey," the ex-boyfriend mumbled upon seeing me.

"Hi?" I asked.

"What's up? So, uh, can the ladies use your bathroom to do their makeup and get ready for the shoot?"

"What shoot?"

"We're shooting our new video on your roof."

"What? Don't you need a permit for that or something?"

"I don't know. Yeah. Probably."

"Wait, what type of video is this? Is anyone gonna be naked?"

"Noooo," he laughed, and then walked out of the apartment and up to my roof. "Noooo" clearly meant "What the hell do you think?"

The tattooed band + 3 strippers + a video camera – permission to use the roof. In the minds of most landlords, that equals eviction.

A few heated phone conversations between my roommate and me later, I was able to put a stop to the production of the video, but the whole process also halted the work I was supposed to be doing that day. It wasn't fair for me to have to clean up someone else's mess, a mess that conceivably could've gotten us fined or, even worse, evicted. And why was she giving our keys out to the lead singer of a punk band? This was a guy who wore a dog collar around his neck.

I was made to feel particularly unsafe thanks to another roommate when I came home late to a wide-open apartment door. I tiptoed into our kitchen and was shocked to find broken glass covering the floor. When I switched on the light, I noticed that one of my roommates had drawn up DANGER signs (complete with skull and crossbones graphics) and taped them around the room. Although I wasn't exactly the model of sobriety myself, I couldn't believe I was living with a person who had chosen to take the time to construct elaborate warning signs rather than clean up the glass. And why the hell was the door wide open? In the morning, my roommate admitted to coming home drunk with a guy who she then had passionate sex with on our kitchen counter. In the heat of the moment, they forgot to close the door behind them and (as if they were in some cheesy late-night Cinemax movie) pushed all the glasses and dishes that were on the countertop onto the floor. "We tried to clean some of the glass up," she said the next morning. "But we didn't have any clothes on, so I thought it was a little dangerous."

"Good thinking," I said. "Much less dangerous to leave the glass on the floor and then turn all the lights off."

All I could think about after getting over the shock of what I'd walked into was how grateful I was that I hadn't walked in on them during the act. My friend Sarah wasn't as fortunate with her roommate, Amber. When Sarah first met Amber in college, she was "all Care Bears and honey," but by the time they moved in together she'd gotten really dark. "She was all gothed out," Sarah said," and she just got darker and darker over time. We lived on the Upper East Side, and she would meet random guys out at bars and go home with them, three to four nights a week." Sarah found Amber's promiscuity sad, but because she was going home with these guys and not bringing them home (Sarah and Amber shared a bedroom), Sarah didn't usually have to see Amber in action. Except once, which Sarah will never forget. "We were out at a bar for her birthday, and my boyfriend and I decided to leave because it was late and we were drunk," Sarah said. "But Amber was flirting with two Swedish guys she'd just met and she didn't want to leave. I didn't feel great about leaving her there alone, but she insisted she'd be fine." About an hour after Sarah and her boyfriend had gotten home, Amber walked in with the two Swedish guys. "We had been asleep, but woke up when we heard them in the living room," she said. "She proceeded to go at it with both of them, and my boyfriend and I could hear everything! I was pissed. I mean, who were these random guys she brought into our apartment? And, ew, she had sex with *both of them* on *our* futon."

The day after the Swedish incident, Sarah threatened to move out if Amber ever brought a strange guy (or *guys*) home again. She never did, and Sarah lived with Amber for six more months, until their lease was up. Amber continued to have sex, but she didn't put Sarah in a position where she had to hear or see it.

Aside from differing opinions on the definition of the term *safe sex*, another problem that can rear its head when it comes to partying in the apartment is the incompatibility between your friends and your roommate's friends. When it comes down to it, if you decide to throw a party, you have to be somewhat accommodating of your roommate. Even if you're not throwing the party together, you can't exclude her or her friends. Maybe they're annoying, maybe your friends don't share the same interests, but you simply can't leave them off the guest list. Sorry, it's just one of the responsibilities of living with roommates.

An acquaintance of mine, Jean, had a roommate who would routinely exclude her and her friends from her parties, particularly her annual Halloween party. "When it came to this bash, she couldn't be stopped," Jean told me. "This girl was super shy, but once a year, she and her wallflower friends would dress up as the slutty ghoul or the slutty princess or the slutty dead bride. Then they'd invite lots of boys over, hang fake cobwebs everywhere, make Jell-O shots, and post RIP signs on the door. Let's just say that Hallmark practically sponsored her party décor."

Jean's roommate and her friends, all around thirty years old, would also set up a keg in the kitchen. "I hadn't seen a keg since college, to be honest," Jean said. "My friends and I, who are all also around thirty, were more into having dinner parties and drinking good wine than throwing keg parties, so in my book, the keg setup seemed odd." During one of these Halloween parties, Jean had some of her friends over to dress up for a loft party they were planning to attend. "My friends and I dressed up in ridiculous costumes, too, but they weren't slutty. When my friends and I came downstairs to grab a drink before the loft party, this whole room of dressed-up introverts stared at us like *we* were the freaks." Jean and her group tried to be polite and mingle, but to no avail. By the time they hit the keg, it got even worse. "My roommate actually had the nerve to ask me to pay for the booze! I told her I'd buy her a six-pack of Pabst Blue Ribbon." Even if Jean's roommate had wanted her to contribute some money to the party, which would already be asking a lot considering she and her friends weren't really even going to be attending it, it was especially rude of her to ask her for it in front of everyone *during* the party. Mostly, though, it made her feel like she was an unwanted guest in her own apartment.

On the opposite end of the spectrum, I had a roommate who was too inviting. She believed that if she was in the mood to "party," everyone else should be as well. Sure, there were times when we all partied together, but she didn't know when to turn the party switch off or, more important, when not to turn it on. For instance, my other roommate and I would feel really uneasy whenever we'd hear her cutting up lines of cocaine on our kitchen counter at 6:00 p.m. "Is that sound what I think it is?" my other roommate would ask, peeking her head into my bedroom. "It can't be," I'd answer. "The sun hasn't even gone down yet." But, alas, it was exactly what we feared it was. What was even worse than her starting her nocturnal activities prematurely was the fact that she wasn't at all discreet about it. She had plenty of counter space in the privacy of her own bedroom, but for some reason she felt the need to advertise her illicit behavior to the rest of the apartment. And the last thing I wanted to see on my way to the gym on a Monday night was my roommate snorting drugs off our kitchen table.

Many times she'd have an accomplice, but when she didn't, she tried to recruit my other roommate and me. "Do you guys want to go in on this with me?" she'd ask.

"No, thanks. Not goin' out tonight," one of us would say.

"Me neither," the other one would chime in.

"Are you guys sure? It's so nice out. Plus, I'm not even gonna stay out late."

The problem with her was that, like most people who want partners in crime, it took her a good fifteen to twenty minutes to accept no as an answer. She tried everything, from offering to pay for our drinks to opening up her enviable closet to us. Finally, when she resigned herself to the fact that we couldn't be persuaded, she'd recruit another friend. On her way out the door, she'd say, "If you guys change your mind, I'll be at the bar around the corner. If I leave there, I'll text you." Then, of course, she'd send a slew of text messages from the bar, letting us know how much fun it was. Good roommates know and accept that no means no. It's exhausting to have to make excuses for not wanting to do drugs or go out. You should try to be perceptive and learn the difference between extending a polite invitation and guilting someone into going out against their will.

The truth is, how you would act while living by yourself is often much different from how you should act while living with others. The people who don't realize this, or who don't care to realize this, will inevitably create discord among their roommates. In fact, it's important to have an almost heightened sense of awareness about what is and is not cool with the people you live with. This isn't to suggest you should walk on eggshells, but it's critical to be very conscious of doing the exact opposite. If possible, it's best to plan parties *with* your roommates, so that all of you have a sense of responsibility for what happens during and after the party, especially when it comes to cleaning up. If your roommates simply don't want to be involved, it's smart to invest in an abundance of heavy-duty trash bags to minimize the amount of postparty cleaning you'll be doing by yourself. It sounds silly, but they've saved me on a number of occasions because when they're strategically placed around the apartment, partygoers actually use them. The cleanup is significantly less painful, and because of that, you're more likely to pick up the remainder of your mess before going to bed, which your roommates will greatly appreciate in the morning.

What's important to remember before moving in with

someone is that they're probably not going to change their habits simply because you don't party as much as they do. "If you move in with a night owl, and you're up at the crack of dawn each day and expect to find harmony, you're in trouble. If you move in with a chronic pot smoker and expect them to blow it all out the window, you're in trouble," explains Dr. Kulic. "If you move in with a constant partier who has a lot of friends and expect them to slow down for you, you're in trouble." Simply put: You'll have to be somewhat prescient. If your roommate is fun and exciting and "always looking for a good time" when you first meet her, think about how that behavior may affect you when you're living with her—when you can't escape it. Dr. Kulic continues, "It's similar to what happens in romantic relationships: The thing that you find most entertaining or endearing about your new boyfriend is the thing that may drive you to the brink of divorce down the road. People often fall in love with people who are different from themselves because they wish to somehow integrate that exciting new personality characteristic into their being." It's often fun to have perpetual partiers as friends; you can choose when and if you want to hang out with them, but being forced into having a "big night" because you live with a perpetual partier is never fun. And listening to her having wild sex is even less fun.

Things to Remember

* Don't have sex on the kitchen table or counter, ever. It's gross.
* Be mindful of the types of guys you bring home.
* By all means, have earth-shattering orgasms, just do it as quietly as possible.
* Know when to turn the party switch off, and when not to turn it on, unless it's done quietly and in the privacy of your own room.
* When throwing any party, buy an abundance of heavy-duty trash bags, and use them throughout the night. And always invite your roommate, even if she might come dressed as a slutty librarian.

Chapter Thirteen
Is That My Underwear You're Wearing?

DO establish rules for sharing clothes.
DON'T stink them up or steal them.

Learning how to share clothes properly is one of the biggest challenges in life for a girl. It's hard to resist the urge to pull your roommate's hair and kick her in the shins when you catch her wearing your brand-new, hasn't-even-been-worn-by-its-owner-yet Marc Jacobs shirt. On the other hand, it's hard to resist sneaking into your roommate's closet and borrowing that brand-new, tags-still-on shirt of hers when you have an event to go to or a hot date that night. Borrowing stuff, often without permission, is an inevitable part of living with girls, and it can also lead to the worst fights a woman will ever endure.

I personally believe that two closets are better than one, so if you can figure out an amicable way to do it, I'm all for roommates leaving the doors to their closets open. Still, rules must be followed, or else you should lock up your closet and hide the key.

I had one roommate who was sneaky about borrowing my clothes. She almost never asked, yet I almost always knew which items she had borrowed. How? Because she never washed or dry-cleaned the items before returning them to my closet. One of the most frustrating feel-ings is trying to get dressed in a hurry and throwing on a top you remember having just cleaned,

Myth: If your roommate happens to be a fashionista with a lot of clothes, she won't notice if you borrow a designer item once in a while.
Fact: If she's a fashionista with a lot of clothes, she's most likely keeping a mental inventory of what's in her closet at all times. Never borrow her clothes without asking. (A fashionista's wrath is not pretty.)

only to arrive at your destination with the realization that you smell like somebody else's B.O. One time I got to work and the smell was so bad that I had to go out and buy another shirt. I was so pissed and disgusted by what my roommate had done to my shirt that I tossed it in the garbage. Looking back, that was probably an extreme move, but I couldn't bear the thought of stuffing the smelly shirt in my bag and then having to wait another eight hours to wash it. Plus, it just wasn't the same shirt anymore. She had marked it as her territory, and there was a good chance that an extra-large cup of Tide wasn't going to change that.[6] I'm sure my roommate didn't think that

---

[6] All day I kept thinking of the *Seinfeld* episode with the valet guy who stinks up Jerry's car with his B.O. When Elaine and Jerry first get in the car, they can't believe the smell. Jerry's confused because the valet guy is gone, but the car still

the shirt smelled as bad as it did when she sneakily hung it back in my closet unwashed, but that's the point: People with a habitual case of B.O. usually don't know that they have B.O. Maybe they don't have sensitive senses of smell, perhaps they think it's everyone around them who smells bad, or most likely it's just that they're immune to their own bad smell. Even if you think that a shirt you've worn all day doesn't smell bad, I guarantee that the person the shirt belongs to will be able to tell that it's been worn by someone other than herself the next time she puts it on. It's an absolute *must* to launder anything you borrow from your roommate's closet, even if you *think* she won't be able to tell that you've worn it.

Another problem I had with the smelly roommate borrowing my clothes was that I didn't get anything in return. While she appreciated nice clothes, she didn't like spending money on acquiring them, so her wardrobe wasn't what I'd call enviable. I, on the other hand, shouldn't have been spending a lot of money on nice clothes, but I often did, which made my closet very tempting to her. I wouldn't have minded sharing my clothes with her *as much* if I had benefited from her closet, but I didn't. Furthermore, she had no incentive to buy nice clothes because she was under the impression that she could just wear the clothes I bought. And when I say "under the impression," I mean that she thought she could borrow my clothes without my finding out about it. (I'd

---

stinks of him. "When somebody has B.O.," Jerry says, "the 'O' usually stays with the 'B.' Once the 'B' leaves, the 'O' goes with it." But as days go by and the smell remains (as strong as ever), they learn that that's not always the case. Which is exactly what I experienced that day.

sometimes ask if she'd worn something of mine, and she'd always deny it.) It was an unfair and frustrating situation for me, and it got to the point where I would hide my nicest pieces just so that she couldn't find them. (Sometimes I'd hide them so well that even *I* couldn't find them.) In this case "the two closets are better than one" rule wasn't applicable because there was only one good closet, and it belonged to me.

Contrarily, two friends of mine who live together are always the best-dressed girls at any event or party because they truly do benefit from the "two closets are better than one" rule. One works in fashion, and the other makes a significant amount of money working in finance. Both of them love nice clothes. The fashionista gets most of her clothes either discounted or for free. She even gets a lot of them months before they hit the stores. The financier can afford to buy whatever designer stuff she wants. By putting their closets together (literally, they share a huge walk-in closet), they've hit the sartorial jackpot, and because they each benefit from the other one's stuff, they have no problem sharing, ever. They also trust each other to take care of the other one's stuff. Their closets are meticulously maintained, and you'll never, for example, find an YSL dress thrown over a chair or a Givenchy blouse crumpled in the corner. Even tops from H&M and the Gap are folded in a store-worthy manner. It's quite beautiful, really.

The stuff they share, though, is limited to dresses, pants, skirts, and tops. "Undergarments are totally off-limits," says my fashion friend. "And with a few exceptions, shoes are too." Shoes can get so easily damaged, especially in a walk-everywhere city like New York, that they're harder to share. (You cut a pair's lifespan almost in half when you share them.) More important, it should be innately understood that you don't wear someone else's underwear or bras. Not only is it unhygienic, but it's creepy and weird. A friend of mine, Candace, was living in Philadelphia with a girl she had known from boarding school when she discovered that this unwritten rule wasn't as universal as she thought. Her room-mate, Demi, had borrowed one of her skirts, which was fine, but when she went into Demi's room to retrieve the skirt, she found it crumpled in the corner, which was absolutely not fine. That was nothing, however, compared with what she was about to discover. "When I picked the skirt up and dusted it off, something fell from my grip," Candace said. "At my feet was a sexy La Perla thong my boyfriend had gotten me for Valentine's Day. And no, it was not clean." Candace was shocked and disgusted, but too embarrassed to confront Demi about it. *Maybe it was a one-time thing*, she hoped.

After the discovery Candace kept her mouth shut but began to keep careful inventory of her underwear supply. "I began to notice that my panties were disappearing," she said. "I would find them stuffed in the back of Demi's closet, under her bed, and when she was feeling careless, just out in the open, lying on her bedroom floor. Sometimes when we were out at night, I'd even recognize a pair peeking out from her low-rise jeans." Candace finally got up the courage to confront Demi. "I didn't accuse her, exactly. I simply asked her if she had seen any of my missing underwear." Demi admitted to nothing, which didn't totally surprise Candace. "After all," said Candace, "she was the type of person who was okay with wearing someone else's underwear." By the time their lease was up, Candace was down to a five-panty rotation, which was significantly less than what she had started with. "That was the last time I ever lived with a girl," Candace said. "Thank God."

Another friend, Anne, was living in Atlanta when she caught her roommate, Jo, in an awkward situation wearing her clothes. "Jo and I had been out together earlier in the night, but I left the bar before her. I went to bed and then heard her return to the apartment about an hour later," Anne told me. "The music went on in her room, and then there was the pitter-patter of feet. It was keeping me awake, so I got up to see what was going on." When Anne tapped on Jo's door, there was no response, so she slowly opened it. Twirling around the room was Jo . . . wearing an entire outfit of Anne's clothes. "She was wearing one of my low-cut shirts and a short skirt of mine, which wasn't what she had worn out that night." In fact, Anne had had no idea these two items were even in Jo's custody. "She noticed me standing there and then immediately crouched down and wrapped her arms around her body, as if I had walked in on her naked." Anne was embarrassed for the both of them. "Oh, oh my God. Sorry," she said, and quickly shut the door. But back in bed Anne had a hard time falling back asleep. "Honestly, I was very confused and a little bit scared for my well-being. I mean, my roommate was dancing around her room by herself in one of my sexy outfits." The next day, Anne asked Jo for her skirt and shirt back, but Jo pretended to have no idea what she was talking about. "You know," Anne pressed, "the outfit you were wearing in your room last night?"

"No, I don't know," Jo insisted.

Anne felt like she was going crazy, but she was positive that she had seen Jo wearing her clothes. "Whenever she left the apartment after that, I'd search her room for the two items. After about a month, I finally found them stuffed in a dusty corner underneath her bathroom sink. I just took them back and never mentioned it again." Anne didn't want to spend all her time interrogating Jo, especially when Jo had vehemently denied it for an entire month, but it certainly made Anne look at her differently. It also made her much more protective of her clothes.

While roommates like Jo and Demi were blatantly stealing—or at least borrowing without permission—other roommates do what I refer to as *politely* steal. They're the girls who borrow one or two items so much that they basically adopt the items as their own. In the beginning they'll ask permission to wear the item, but over time they'll stop returning whatever it is they borrowed right away, or they'll ask to wear the item to work but then take it away with them for a long weekend as well.

One of my roommates, Jamie, loved a mohair sweater I used to own. I didn't particularly like the way it looked, or felt, on me, but it was an impulsive buy and I had paid a lot of money for it. I felt attached, if not obligated, to it. Jamie coveted the sweater so much that I didn't mind lending it to her once in a while. The situation only became a problem when she decided, without my consent, that her closet was a more suitable home for it. Yes, she liked it more than I did, but it was still *my* sweater—an itchy, ill-fitting sweater I paid way too much money for, but still mine—and while I let her borrow it from time to time, she didn't have the right to decide where it should reside. Because I didn't *love* the sweater, it took me a while to notice it was missing from my closet. Once I realized it was gone, I immediately went to her closet, pulled it out, and put it on. I admit that I did this out of spite, but I wanted to set a precedent: She didn't have the right to an item of my clothing simply because she liked it and wore it more than I did. *I have to do this*, I thought, *or the rest of my closet is at stake.* As soon as I put the sweater on, not only did I notice that it smelled like her perfume, but it was stretched out at the neck, some of the threads were pulled, and there was a hole in the armpit. *Shit, now I can't even sell it to a consignment shop*, I thought. I promised myself that I'd wear the sweater as long as the weather and my skin permitted, which turned out to be exactly forty-five minutes.

"Aren't you hot in that?" my other roommate, Samantha, asked when she saw me.

"A little bit," I conceded.

"Why are you wearing it then? And anyway, isn't it Jamie's sweater?"

"No. It's mine, and it was really expensive!"

"Whoa. Okaaay."

I was so frustrated that I went back into my room, yanked the sweater off, and stuffed it in a bag of clothes I had been planning to drop off at Goodwill for months. Later that week, I made my Goodwill donation—mohair sweater and all. When Jamie asked to wear the sweater again, I lied and said, "Sorry, I'm planning on wearing it tonight."

I know it was childish to give the sweater away rather than give it to the person who loved it so much, but I didn't like the way she had just taken it from me. I wanted to get back at her for taking advantage of my generosity (again, I know, an incredibly petty move). I did have a right to be upset at the way she had "borrowed" it, but I should've handled things differently too. Confronting her directly could've yielded much better results for the both of us. For example, offering to sell her the sweater for half of what I paid for it would have benefited both her and me. It also would've been a clear way to let her know that she couldn't just take anything from my closet without (a) asking to borrow it or (b) paying for it. Dr. Kulic says, "It's difficult to tell someone no when they ask to borrow something, but problems arise when there are no limits set. Like many other situations, you won't know someone is a chronic borrower/stealer until she's already committing the crime, but sometimes the best way to deal with these situations is to head them off at the pass with clear communication." Dr. Kulic suggests saying something like this to your roommate: "Sure, you can borrow my shirt, but I'd really like it back tomorrow." Rather than leave it up to her to return it "on time," just tell her when you expect the item to be returned.

Another difficult aspect of sharing clothes is the size factor—when roommates are close enough in size to share *some* clothes but not close enough in size to share *all* clothes. Samantha, the roommate that Jamie and I lived with, had a problem facing the fact that she had gained fifteen pounds in six months. When we first moved in together, she and I wore the same jean size, so we shared jeans all the time. Once she got a new, more demanding job, she had less time to work out and more time to sit around and eat. The weight gain depressed her so much that she went into full denial mode. Rather than buy bigger jeans or start working out more, she squeezed herself into the clothes she wore when she was fifteen pounds skinnier, including *my jeans.* We still shared things like jackets and tops, but sharing with her became a big problem for me, because while I didn't want to make her feel bad about the weight she had gained, I'd be lying if I said I didn't die a little inside every time I saw her squeezed into my size 27 Paper Denims. When we were both the same size, I had no problem keeping my jean drawer open for her, mainly because I was also benefiting from the deal. The deal, of course, didn't work so well for me when she gained weight because she was stretching out the seams on *all* our jeans.

For months, I struggled over what to do. Then I inadvertently solved the problem. At a sample sale one day, I came across a pair of Earnest Sewn jeans. They were a size too big, but ridiculously cheap, so I couldn't pass them up. *Good for lounging around in on the weekend*, I thought. When I got home and added them to my beloved jean drawer, it hit me: *Also good for Samantha's butt!* I didn't have her in mind when I bought them, but when I offered to let her wear them one day, she loved them—so much so that she began to wear them more than any of our other jeans. (I think the relief of putting on a pair of jeans that were not too tight after six months of wearing jeans that gave her a muffin top was a euphoric experience for her.) Samantha eventually lost the weight, and those Earnest Sewn jeans have a place of honor in my drawer to this day.

Things to Remember

* Assess the benefit of sharing closets with your roommate (e.g., do you shop at similar stores and wear the same designers?). Create rules if this seems like something that would benefit the both of you.
* Clean every piece of borrowed clothing before returning it. (Consult her on how she likes to care for each particular item first, though. Some people, for

example, refuse to put their jeans in the dryer.)
* Envy your roommate's body, but don't think that
  squeezing yourself into her jeans is going to give it to
  you.
* Undergarments and shoes are always off-limits.

Chapter Fourteen

Uh, I Think You Forgot Your Pants

DO feel comfortable with your body.
DON'T expect your roommate to feel comfortable
with it if it's not clothed.

The nudity issue is a complicated one. People should feel comfortable in their homes, yes, but complete comfort is unfortunately one of the things we sacrifice when we have roommates, so if you're thinking about walking around nude in your apartment because you feel clothes are too restrictive, you might want to consider the fact that you're running the risk of scarring your roommates for life. "From the get-go," says Dr. Lewis, "you must decide with your roommate what type of nudity should be allowed in the apartment."

One of my roommates loved to do everything naked: cook naked, sit on the kitchen counter and chat naked, watch TV naked, read naked, talk on the phone naked, and so forth. It was uncomfortable for me, mainly because I didn't know where to look and—let's face it—a person can't help but look. What I found most disconcerting was her tendency to wear nothing but a T-shirt. Underwear and no shirt: tolerable (comparatively). A T-shirt and no underwear: pretty weird. The fact that she actually took the time to put on a T-shirt suggested that clothing had in fact been on her mind before she walked out of the privacy of her own bedroom. It wasn't like, "Oops! I forgot to put any clothes on." Instead, it was, "Look! I haven't gotten a bikini wax in six months!" She was so casual about her nudity that I'd often do double takes when I saw her. Actually, they were more like involuntary twitches: I didn't

> **Myth:** If you're used to walking around your apartment nude or in itsy-bitsy underwear, you shouldn't have to change that simply because you acquire a roommate.
> **Fact:** Too much information shown physically is just as bad as too much information given verbally, and it can make your roommate so uncomfortable she'll try to avoid you as much as possible.

want to look again, but it was as if my brain needed to confirm that a nude person had in fact just walked by me and waved hello. It's not that I have a phobia of the nude body; it's just that there's a time and a place to be naked, and I'm not the type of person who likes to engage in girl talk when the person I'm talking with isn't wearing clothes. I think the majority of people are probably in my corner on that matter.[7] Not surprisingly, my always-naked

---

[7] In one *Seinfeld* episode Jerry starts dating a woman who loves to do everything naked, forcing him to distinguish between good naked and bad naked. "Naked hair brushing, good; naked crouching, bad." People, especially your roommates, have a threshold for how and when they can see you nude, so try to limit it to only the necessary times.

roommate was frequently "getting caught" in the nude by our guests, which was pretty awkward (especially if the guest happened to be one of my boyfriends, who always did double takes too, thought I'm not sure if they were voluntary or involuntary).

I was shocked by my roommate's affinity for walking around the apartment nude, but she may have been shocked by the amount of unease it caused me. Before I moved in with her, I assumed everyone felt the way I did about public nudity, which is why Dr. Lewis says roommates "should never make assumptions. Express your feelings from the very beginning." If I had told my roommate that it'd make me feel better if she threw some underwear on before leaving the privacy of her room, I probably could've spared myself a lot of uncomfortable situations. "Nudity is a great example of how most of us are raised in different home environments," says Dr. Kulic. "Comfort around the home is a very important issue for people. We often spend so much time dressed up to do one thing or another that home is the one place we want to just let our hair down and take our pants off. There's nothing inherently wrong with getting completely naked and sitting with a tub of ice cream in front of the TV for several hours—if you live alone. Modern rules of decency, however, tend to contradict this type of behavior when other people are around. [As a roommate,] you have to learn to be considerate of others' preferences, even if they are not your own. Perhaps you have no idea why someone might be uncomfortable around nudity, but a considerate person tries to be less concerned with why and more concerned with how to help out."

A colleague of mine, Darlene, can relate to the embarrassment an always-naked roommate can cause. She was living with a girl in New York who was going away for the summer. "My roommate said she looked long and hard [on Craigslist] to find a suitable person to take her place," Darlene said. Finally, she interviewed a girl over the phone and decided she'd be a good fit. They wouldn't find out until after the girl moved in that she was probably naked during the interview. "About a month after the interview, the girl, Gabriel, arrived from Miami at 6:30 a.m. on a Sunday," Darlene told me. "When I answered the door, I was in my full bedtime glory: ragged tee, boxer shorts, probably even some pimple cream on my face." What stood in front of Darlene was the exact opposite: "Gabriel's huge, fake breasts were bulging out of her denim jumpsuit, and she had on enough makeup to make Tammy Faye jealous. Her eye shadow was practically up to her forehead and she had these red, red lips. I was taken aback, but her soft voice and sweet demeanor reminded me not to judge a book by its cover."

Unfortunately, that cover became more difficult not to judge as the day went on. "After Gabriel unpacked, she told me she was going to the park to relax. Now, most people put on a bathing suit, a tank top, and a pair of shorts to do something like that, but not Gabriel. She applied even more makeup and changed into a long, black, sleeveless V-neck dress that looked like something Stevie Nicks would've worn in the seventies." Very strange, yes, but not yet offensive.

Darlene only started to be bothered by Gabriel's weird taste when she began to walk around the apartment naked. "Remember, this was *my* apartment," Darlene said, "and I certainly didn't want some other person sitting on my couch bare-assed." One time, after a long day of work, Darlene opened the door to her apartment and noticed something move suddenly. "As I walked in, I realized it was Gabriel's bare ass scampering from the kitchen, where she was cooking, to her bedroom. Ew." It should be noted here that Gabriel's ass was almost impossible to miss. "As beautiful as her skin was," Darlene noted, "it was pretty much albino-white." Darlene and Gabriel exchanged nervous laughs, but when Gabriel re-emerged from her room, she came out wrapped in only a sheer sarong. "Not much better. Plus, I couldn't help but wonder, who cooks naked? Wasn't she afraid of splattering grease on certain body parts?"

Gabriel's propensity for walking around naked continued to make Darlene feel uncomfortable, and the problem came to an embarrassing head when Darlene's parents were in town one weekend. "I purposely called Gabriel thirty minutes before we arrived to let her know I would be coming back to the apartment with my parents. I wanted to make sure she was wearing appropriate clothing. I even faux fumbled with the keys once I got to the front door so that she'd hear us and put something on, but lo and behold, when I opened the door, my whole family got a glimpse of her alabaster behind." Gabriel bolted to her room as soon as she saw Darlene's parents. "But what was she wearing when she came back out to say hi? Just that sheer sarong again." Maybe Gabriel had exhibitionist tendencies, or perhaps she was simply more comfortable being nude all the time. Either way, she should've suppressed those desires while living with a roommate. "I mean, what was up with her always lying on the couch naked when she knew I was coming home?" Darlene asked. "Honestly, I know it's mean to say, but I was glad to get rid of her at the end of the summer."

Darlene didn't expect Gabriel to dress as if the apartment were a church, but she also didn't want her to treat it like it was a nudist colony. Gabriel's nudity made Darlene uncomfortable in general, but the places she chose to be nude in (namely, the kitchen and on the couch) particularly grossed her out.

Another friend, Sari, was also severely grossed out by her always-naked roommate, Carrie, when she walked in on her committing an act not suitable for the kitchen: giving herself a Brazilian bikini wax. "I opened the door to my apartment," Sari said, "and there was my roommate, naked in the kitchen, on the phone, with one leg on the countertop, and a bowl of hot wax next to her." Carrie didn't even flinch when she saw Sari. Holding the phone to her ear with her right shoulder, she chirped "hey" to Carrie, continued to talk to whomever it was she was talking to, and started to apply hot wax to her nether regions. "I couldn't believe that (a) she was completely naked in our kitchen (b) she was giving *herself* a Brazilian bikini wax and (c) she was talking on the phone while doing it," Sari said. "I almost threw up."

Pubic hair and hot wax are forbidden in the kitchen, especially if you're sharing that kitchen with another person. After Sari went into her bedroom and gathered her thoughts, she knew she had to put a stop to what was happening right next to her silverware and Kellogg's Corn Flakes. She shifted into emergency mode and re-entered the kitchen, where Carrie was still on the phone, and angrily mouthed, "Carrie. What are you doing?"

"What?" Carrie asked, confused.

"Um . . . ," Sari said. Her eyes widened as she looked around the kitchen and then back at the hot wax to emphasize the grossness of the combination. Carrie still didn't get it.

"What?" she asked again. (Surely, Sari thought, whoever was on the other line with Carrie couldn't have known what was going on.) "Mom, lemme call you back. This wax is sticking to everything."

Sari's jaw dropped. "You're talking to your mom?"

"Yeah, what's up?" She asked as she hung up the phone.

"Well, don't you think it's a little gross to be waxing yourself in the kitchen? *Our* kitchen?"

"Oh. Ha. Sorry. I didn't think you'd care." She giggled as she stirred the wax.

"You know, there are places you can go where they'll do that for you," Sari said.

But Carrie just laughed again and continued to stir

the wax. After that night, and one more explanation from Sari about why pubic hair and food don't go together, Carrie agreed to keep her hot wax and naked body out of the kitchen. She moved her one-woman waxing operation to the bathroom instead. "It was still weird to me that she gave herself her own Brazilian bikini waxes, but at least I didn't have to see it," Sari said.

Another friend, Adrian, was sharing an apartment in LA when her roommate decided to get in touch with her exhibitionist side (and yes, that's putting it euphemistically). "My roommate, Pamela, was a smart girl who worked a bunch of jobs, earned scholarships, and had aspirations to be a film executive," Adrian said. "But after answering an ad in our local weekly paper, she started working at a video distribution center for porn." The job paid well and Pamela began attending "porn parties" in big houses in the Seminal Valley. "She then started doing topless photo shoots and eventually moved on to live-action sex films." This was certainly a disturbing sequence of events, but Adrian tried not to judge . . . until Pamela's magazines started showing up all over the apartment. "Porn magazines, with her vagina in a centerfold, would be sitting right next to my *Us Weekly*s," Adrian said. "Pamela would then ask me how she looked in these photos. I mean, how do you objectively review your roommate lying naked on a stack of hay? I always just told her she had a nice wax. I'm not kidding. That's all I could say."

Not only did Adrian have to deal with seeing Pamela

in these X-rated photos, but she got to see the in-the-flesh version as well. "Pamela was about six feet tall and stacked like an IHOP breakfast," Adrian said. "In the apartment she would walk around in bras and teeny, tiny workout clothes. If a guy—any guy—happened to be coming over, she would always throw on the same outfit: short shorts, a white tank top, and no bra, which was lethal at her DD status. It was sad, though, because I knew her clothes getting smaller was a direct correlation to her shrinking self-esteem."

Adrian and Pamela ended their roommate relationship amicably, but because of the drastically different directions their lives went in they never talk or see each other anymore. Would it have helped if Adrian had tried to talk to Pamela about her nudity? Possibly, but Pamela seemed set on her new career path. However, most roommates don't harbor aspirations of becoming porn stars and therefore might appreciate you honestly discussing your feelings about how many articles of clothing is the bare minimum before entering the kitchen or sitting down on the communal couch.

Things to Remember

* Always opt for bottoms first. There's just something about walking around with no underwear on that doesn't work when you're living with someone who isn't either your boyfriend or Winnie the Pooh.
* Make an effort to be properly clothed when your roommate is entertaining a male guest. Even if you

think wearing a sheer top with no bra and itsy-bitsy shorts is completely acceptable, believe me, your roommates think otherwise.

* If you live with a roommate who treats your apartment like a nudist colony, and it makes you uncomfortable, politely ask her to at least wear a bathrobe or a long T-shirt, something that'll appease you and that doesn't require too much effort on her part.

Chapter Fifteen
Seeking What?!

DO pay attention to the language used in
"Roommate Wanted" classified ads.
DON'T believe everything you read.

The best way to determine whether a rental market is out of control is by perusing the room/share section of a site like Craigslist: The more ridiculous the demands in the Roommate Wanted listings, the higher the occupancy rate in that city. As the occupancy rate rises, people with apartments to share become more draconian (and just plain odd) in their postings. It goes way beyond "seeking professional SWF" territory and enters the "seeking spiritually like-minded, comic-book enthusiast and antique-lover" zone. Are these people looking for roommates or their long-lost twins? In a place like Manhattan, with an outrageous number of people *seeking* rooms to rent, the ones *renting* the rooms have the freedom to be frighteningly specific about what they expect from their potential roommates. And anyone with a lot of suitors always risks abusing her power.

When looking for a place to live, you should be circumspect about a classified ad that makes unusual and unrealistic demands. At first glance you may think the person who posted the ad included such a long list of demands as a way to weed out the crazies, but their demands often reveal just how crazy *they* are. It's possible that the person who posts an ad with an extralong list of demands is expecting to mold you into her perfect little roommate doll. As a helpful exercise, take a look at the following posts I spotted on Craigslist: "Doesn't bring the party home, clean, pays rent on time, considerate and laid-back." This person lists simple, short, and to-the-point demands. He or she says, "Here's basically what I'm looking for, let's meet and see how we like each other." As opposed to this one: "Two French roommates who are very liberal, socially active, looking for someone who isn't allergic to smoke." ("Isn't allergic to smoke"? What does that even mean? They don't care if you're a nonsmoker and that smoke bothers you, as long as you don't have a seizure from their six-pack-a-day habit?); or this: "Ashram-like accommodations for the months of May

> **Myth:** If a city's occupancy rate is at 99 percent, you must resign yourself to living with someone you may not like in an apartment that totally sucks.
> **Fact:** As the occupancy rate in a city rises, it's harder to find a good apartment with a roommate who has reasonable expectations, but with some work, it can be done.

and June on the Upper West Side." Uh . . . what? The one person I know who went to an ashram lost ten pounds in a week
and did enough journal writing to last her for the rest of her
life. And, as if that isn't enough to deter you, Dictionary.com's
definition of an ashram is this: "a secluded building, often the
residence of a guru, used for religious retreat or instruction
in Hinduism." This sounds very much like a euphemism for
"shitty apartment with no amenities." This same classified
goes on to say, "If you have a skill in some form of spa treatments, yoga, massage, makeup, alternative health, alternative
healing, and are interested in making money, even better."
So . . . basically, you have the option of getting paid to per-
form any number of obscure spa treatments on people—your
roommate, probably—while in the comfort of your own home.
Sounds great! Another couple of girls in San Francisco were
looking for a roommate who didn't have "a passive/aggressive
personality," which is a normal thing to want, even though
nobody ever thinks of themselves as passive aggressive, so
it's not really even worth mentioning. (There's also no point in
posting something like this: "Crazy people need not apply."
Again, nobody crazy ever thinks they're crazy. That's part of
what makes them crazy.) These girls then go on to say, "We
prefer meat eaters," which seemed a little strange to me. I
eat meat, but of all the things I look for in a roommate, "meat
eater" is not even close to the top of the list. Perhaps these
girls both had bad experiences living with vegetarians in the
past, but as long as their new roommate doesn't gag at the

sight of meat or proselytize about the cruelty of eating meat, I don't see why non—meat eaters and meat eaters can't live harmoniously together, unless something else is going on, like raw-meat breakfast buffets in the kitchen every morning.

Another eyebrow-raising classified started off like this: "$1600 large room available for female in Greenwich Village." Sounds great, until . . . "I have the best dog in the whole world, his name is M and he is a big boy but he thinks he is small. He is a black lab/great dane mix and NEVER barks and pretty much sleeps on his bed in the living room unless he's feeling playful in which case he might bring you a toy or two just to show you." Okay, unless this dog is on some serious sedatives, I find it hard to believe he *never* barks or wants to do more than just *show* people his toys. A little more worrisome is the fact that rather than post any photos of the apartment, she posted three big pictures of the dog—her very *big* dog. Sure, her dog may be lovable and sweet, but at his size, you're pretty much moving into an apartment with two roommates, not one, and it sounds a lot like the dog probably gets the run of the house. Plus, if he "thinks he is small" but is actually the size of a small horse, what does that mean for your safety? This isn't necessarily a run-the-other-way posting, but it's one you'd probably want to think twice about before responding to.

Something else to watch out for in these postings is how people describe themselves. If they get too detailed about their interests, they probably want you to have most of the same ones. Also, too many disparate and wacky interests in one person can reveal some mental instability in them. Take this seeker's description, for example: "Ivy League grad, professional actor and life coach, spiritually grounded, avid comic book collector, huge NFL fan." First of all, "Ivy League grad"? Mentioning that seems a bit pretentious. Second, the juxtaposition of "spiritually grounded" and "huge NFL fan" makes me nervous. And while "huge NFL fan" is useful information by itself—be prepared to surrender the couch on Sundays and Monday nights—"spiritually grounded" is just a little too much information. In a separate classified, two girls in San Francisco who were looking for a female roommate described themselves like this: "We have both been deemed 'anal' by others," and they want a roommate "who gets excited by common areas that are neat." The fact that these girls admit that others see them as anal, as if it's a good thing, is a little scary. "Neat" is positive, "anal" is not. And while there are a lot of things to get *excited* about in an apartment (a washer and dryer, for example, or a big bathroom), a neat common area isn't really one of them. I can't even imagine what these girls do for fun, besides maybe stay up late "on school nights" to organize their *Martha Stewart Living* magazines. One of the girls goes on to say this about herself: "My friends describe me as sassy and sarcastic. If you're neither, we'll probably get along," which sounds more like a threat than a description of who she is. And can someone really be anal *and* sassy? I think they kinda cancel each other out. Another person was looking for a "really laid-back spiritual female." It then says, "I have spiritual art in almost every room, so please be okay with that." Exactly what type of spiritual art isn't specified, so even if you are a "really laid-back spiritual female," it'll probably be hard for either one of you to stay laid-back if you're both really spiritual but believe in different spirits.

And like most profiles on a dating site, Roommate Wanted classified ads don't usually give an accurate description of the apartment. You can probably bet that the apartment will not measure up to how it's described in the posting. I know that sounds pessimistic, but my experience has taught me that just as people frequently shave off a few pounds when divulging their weight, they also tend to embellish in classifieds. Here's a crash course in decoding the listings: "Cozy" means smaller than normal, "very spacious" means not tiny, "sun-drenched" means it doesn't face a brick wall, and "has character" means very old with a lot of leaks. Also, be wary of postings that are replete with exclamation points and that have too many specific demands or effusive descriptions. Occasionally, you may be pleasantly surprised by an apartment's appearance, but as a rule of thumb, it's always best to lower your expectations before seeing a place.

Ultimately, the classifieds you should be responding to are the ones that sound the most realistic and are written in a straightforward manner (and while they're a tad harder to find, they are out there). Just because the occupancy rate is at, say, 99 percent in your city doesn't mean you should settle for a roommate who wants you to morph into her soul mate or make spiritual art with her. You also shouldn't settle for a crappy room in an overpriced apartment. Compromising on certain things is a must, but if you're willing to put the work into carefully reading through postings and asking around (put the word out through coworkers, friends, relatives, or anyone you know who may know someone living in the city you live in or want to move to), opportunities will present themselves to you. You then must use your judgment to sift through those opportunities, and lo and behold, you may just find the perfect roommate waiting for you in the perfect apartment . . . or at least a reasonably sane roommate in a "sun-drenched" apartment with not too much "character."

Things to Remember

* Always be wary of signs in a classified ad that a roommate seeker is overcompensating for something (exclamation points, too-good-to-be-true descriptions, and odd demands).
* Pay attention to the way in which a person describes herself in a posting. Weird and disparate characteristics may be a sign of mental instability.
* Lower your expectations before meeting a potential roommate or seeing an apartment. The people who post the ads frequently embellish.

Epilogue

While this book is chock-full of horror stories, it doesn't mean that living with roommates has to be like living in one long, scary movie. Some of the most fun times of my life were spent with my roommates. And my girlfriends (some of whom are ex-roommates) and I love to laugh about our past living situations, even the ones that weren't so funny at the time.

Whatever the case, whether these situations were fun or stressful, they affected us to the point of change. We learned to be forgiving without being pushovers. We learned to be open while still respecting boundaries. And we learned that there are more definitions of the word *party* than we could ever have imagined, thanks to our roommates who had interesting ideas about how to have a good time. These lessons have helped us not only deal with roommates, they've improved the way we interact with people in general. Our relationships, in all areas of our lives, are better because of what we went through while living with roommates.

The twenties can be a very stressful decade—probably *the* most stressful. We're trying to figure out so many things—our career paths, how close or far we want to be to our families, what type of people we'd consider settling down with, and whether or not we even want to settle down, ever. Having roommates during that decade in our lives can be both helpful and debilitating; we're living with people who are facing many of the same obstacles and stresses, which can make us feel less alone and give us a sense of camaraderie, but those same people may choose to deal with these stresses in vastly different ways than we do, which can present a lot of the problems illustrated in this book.

Today, I can laugh at many of my past experiences, and I'm also genuinely thankful for them, even the bad ones. Would I have made some different decisions had I known the things I know now? Sure. And hopefully you'll benefit from my hindsight. Yet even as a guide, this book is still not always going to save you from annoying, sometimes crazy, roommates. If it makes you feel better, we often grow the most when we're put in uncomfortable situations, when we're taken out of our comfort zone and put in a place that challenges our views and beliefs. In the best instances, those views and beliefs change for the better.

While I no longer live with girl roommates today, I do have a new kind of roommate—a live-in boyfriend. Some of the lessons I learned while living with girls has helped me be a more tolerant and better roommate to him. He, on the other hand, has a few things to work on. But that's a whole other book.

About the Author

Amy Zalneraitis lives in Manhattan and writes for various lifestyle/fashion publications. She's no longer seeking roommates, except ones of the four-legged variety who occasionally bark. This is her first book.

Printed in the United States
By Bookmasters